I0670761

THE DOOMSWOMAN

An Historical Romance of Old California

GERTRUDE ATHERTON

1st WORLD
LIBRARY
Literary Society

The Doomswoman

Gertrude Franklin Horn Atherton

© 1st World Library, 2007
PO Box 2211
Fairfield, IA 52556
www.1stworldlibrary.com
First Edition

LCCN: 2007930786

Softcover ISBN: 978-1-4218-4829-7
Hardcover ISBN: 978-1-4218-4732-0
eBook ISBN: 978-1-4218-4926-3

Purchase *"The Doomswoman"*
as a traditional bound book at:
www.1stWorldLibrary.com/purchase.asp?ISBN=978-1-4218-4829-7

1st World Library is a literary, educational organization
dedicated to:

- Creating a free internet library of downloadable ebooks

- Hosting writing competitions and offering book publishing
scholarships.

Interested in more 1st World Library books? contact:
literacy@1stworldlibrary.com
Check us out at: www.1stworldlibrary.com

1ˢᵗ World Library Literary Society

Giving Back to the World

"If you want to work on the core problem, it's early school literacy."

- James Barksdale, former CEO of Netscape

"No skill is more crucial to the future of a child, or to a democratic and prosperous society, than literacy."

- Los Angeles Times

"Literacy... means far more than learning how to read and write... The aim is to transmit... knowledge and promote social participation."

- UNESCO

"Literacy is not a luxury, it is a right and a responsibility. If our world is to meet the challenges of the twenty-first century we must harness the energy and creativity of all our citizens."

- President Bill Clinton

"Parents should be encouraged to read to their children, and teachers should be equipped with all available techniques for teaching literacy, so the varying needs and capacities of individual kids can be taken into account."

- Hugh Mackay

To

STEPHEN FRANKLIN

I

It was at Governor Alvarado's house in Monterey that Chonita first knew of Diego Estenega. I had told him much of her, but had never cared to mention the name of Estenega in the presence of an Iturbi y Moncada.

Chonita came to Monterey to stand godmother to the child of Alvarado and of her friend Dona Martina, his wife. She arrived the morning before the christening, and no one thought to tell her that Estenega was to be godfather. The house was full of girls, relatives of the young mother, gathered for the ceremony and subsequent week of festivities. Benicia, my little one, was at the rancho with Ysabel Herrera, and I was staying with the Alvarados. So many were the guests that Chonita and I slept together. We had not seen each other for a year, and had so much to say that we did not sleep at all. She was ten years younger than I, but we were as close friends as she with her alternate frankness and reserve would permit. But I had spent several months of each year since childhood at her home in Santa Barbara, and I knew her better than she knew herself; when, later, I read her journal, I found little in it to surprise me, but much to fill and cover with shapely form the skeleton of the story which passed in greater part before my eyes.

We were discussing the frivolous mysteries of dress, if I

remember aright, when she laid her hand on my mouth suddenly.

"Hush!" she said.

A caballero serenaded his lady at midnight in Monterey.

The tinkle of a guitar, the jingling of spurs, fell among the strong tones of a man's voice.

Chonita had been serenaded until she had fled to the mountains for sleep, but she crept to the foot of the bed and knelt there, her hand at her throat. A door opened, and, one by one, out of the black beyond, five white-robed forms flitted into the room. They looked like puffs of smoke from a burning moon. The heavy wooden shutters were open, and the room was filled with cold light.

The girls waltzed on the bare floor, grouped themselves in mock-dramatic postures, then, overcome by the strange magnetism of the singer, fell into motionless attitudes, listening intently. How well I remember that picture, although I have almost forgotten the names of the girls!

In the middle of the room two slender figures embraced each other, their black hair falling loosely over their white gowns. On the window-step knelt a tall girl, her head pensively supported by her hand, a black shawl draped gracefully about her; at her feet sat a girl with head bowed to her knees. Between the two groups was a solitary figure, kneeling with hand pressed to the wall and face uplifted.

When the voice ceased I struck a match, and five pairs of little hands applauded enthusiastically. He sang them another song, then galloped away.

Gertrude Franklin Horn Atherton

"It is Don Diego Estenega," said one of the girls. "He rarely sings, but I have heard him before."

"An Estenega!" exclaimed Chonita.

"Yes; of the North, thou knowest. His Excellency thinks there is no man in the Californias like him,—so bold and so smart. Thou rememberest the books that were burned by the priests when the governor was a boy, because he had dared to read them, no? Well, when Diego Estenega heard of that, he made his father send to Boston and Mexico for those books and many more, and took them up to his redwood forests in the north, far away from the priests. And they say he had read other books before, although such a lad; his father had brought them from Spain, and never cared much for the priests. And he has been to Mexico and America and Europe! God of my soul! it is said that he knows more than his Excellency himself,—that his mind works faster. Ay! but there was a time when he was wild,—when the mescal burnt his throat like hornets and the aguardiente was like scorpions in his brain; but that was long ago, before he was twenty; now he is thirty-four. He amuses himself sometimes with the girls,—*valgame Dios!* he has made hot tears flow,—but I suppose we do not know enough for him, for he marries none. Ay! but he has a charm."

"Like what does he look? A beautiful caballero, I suppose, with eyes that melt and a mouth that trembles like a woman in the palsy."

"Ay, no, my Chonita; thou art wrong. He is not beautiful at all. He is rather haggard, and wears no mustache, and he has the profile of the great man, fine and aquiline and severe, excepting when he smiles, and then sometimes he looks kind and sometimes he looks like a devil. He has not the beauty of color; his hair is brown, I think, and his eyes are gray, and set far back; but how they flash! I think they could burn if they looked too long. He is tall and straight and very strong, not so indolent as most of our men. They call him The American because he moves so quickly and gets so cross when people do not think fast enough. *He* thinks like lightning strikes. Ay! they all say that he will be governor in his time; that he would have been long ago, but he has been away so much. It must be that he has seen and admired thee, my Chonita, and discovered thy grating. Thou art happy that thou too hast read the books. Thou and he will be great friends, I know!"

"Yes!" exclaimed Chonita, scornfully. "It is likely. Thou hast forgotten—perhaps—the enmity between the Capulets and the Montagues was a sallow flame to the bitter hatred, born of jealousy in love, politics, and social precedence, which exists between the Estenegas and the Iturbi y Moncadas?"

II

Delfina, the first child of Alvarado, born in the purple at the governor's mansion in Monterey, was about to be baptized with all the pomp and ceremony of the Church and time. Dona Martina, the wife of a year, was unable to go to the church, but lay beneath her lace and satin coverlet, her heavy black hair half covering the other side of the bed. Beside her stood the nurse, a fat, brown, high-beaked old crone, holding a mass of grunting lace. I stood at the foot of the bed, admiring the picture.

"Be careful for the sun, Tomasa," said the mother. "Her eyes must be strong, like the Alvarados',—black and keen and strong."

"Sure, senora."

"And let her not smother, nor yet take cold. She must grow tall and strong,—like the Alvarados."

"Sure, senora."

"Where is his Excellency?"

"I am here." And Alvarado entered the room. He looked amused, and probably had overheard the conversation. He justified, however, the admiration of his young wife. His tall military figure had the perfect poise and suggestion of power natural to a man whose genius had been recognized by the Mexican government before he had entered his twenties. The clean-cut face, with its calm profile and fiery eyes, was not that of the Washington of his emulation, and I never understood why he chose so tame a model. Perhaps because of the meagerness of that early proscribed literature; or did the title "Father of his Country" appeal irresistibly to that lofty and doomed ambition?

He passed his hand over his wife's long white fingers, but did not offer her any other caress in my presence.

"How dost thou feel?"

"Well; but I shall be lonely. Do not stay long at the church, no? How glad I am that Chonita came in time for the christening! What a beautiful *comadre* she will be! I have just seen her. Ay, poor Diego! he will fall in love with her; and what then?"

"It would have been better had she come too late, I think. To avoid asking Diego to stand for my first child was impossible, for he is the man of men to me. To avoid asking Dona Chonita was equally impossible, I suppose, and it will be painful for both. He serenaded her last night, not knowing who she was, but having seen her at her grating; he only returned yesterday. I hope she plants no thorns in his heart."

"Perhaps they will marry and bind the wounds," suggested the woman.

"An Estenega and an Iturbi y Moncada will not marry. He might forget, for he is passionate and of a nature to break down barriers when a wish is dear; but she has all the wrongs of all the Iturbi y Moncadas on her white shoulders, and all their pride in the carriage of her head; to say nothing of that brother whom she adores. She learned this morning that it was Diego's determined opposition that kept Reinaldo out of the Departmental Junta, and meets him in no tender frame of mind—"

Dona Martina raised her hand. Chonita stood in the doorway. She was quite beautiful enough to plant thorns where she listed. Her tall supple figure was clothed in white, and over her gold hair—lurid and brilliant, but without a tinge of red—she wore a white lace mantilla. Her straight narrow brows and heavy lashes were black; but her skin was more purely white than her gown. Her nose was finely cut, the arch almost indiscernible, and she had the most sculptured mouth I have ever seen. Her long eyes were green, dark, and luminous. Sometimes they had the look of a child, sometimes she allowed them to flash with the fire of an animated spirit. But the expression she chose to cultivate was that associated with crowned head and sceptered hand; and sure no queen had ever looked so calm, so inexorable, so haughty, so terribly clear of vision. She never posed—for any one, at least, but herself. For some reason—a youthful reason probably—the iron in her nature was most admired by her. Wherefore,—also, as she had the power, as twin, to heal and curse,—I had named her the Doomswoman, and by this name she was known far and wide. By the lower class of Santa Barbara she was called The Golden Senorita, on account of her hair and of her father's vast wealth.

"Come," she said, "every one is waiting. Do not you hear the voices?"

The windows were closed, but through them came a murmur like that of a pine forest.

The governor motioned to the nurse to follow Chonita and myself, and she trotted after us, her ugly face beaming with pride of position. Was not in her arms the oldest-born of a new generation of Alvarados? the daughter of the governor of The Californias? Her smock, embroidered with silk, was new, and looked whiter than fog against her bare brown arms and face. Her short red satin skirt, a gift of her happy lady's, was the finest ever worn by exultant nurse. About her stringy old throat was a gold chain, bright red roses were woven in her black reboso. I saw her admire Chonita's stately figure with scornful reserve of the colorless gown.

We were followed in a moment by the governor, adjusting his collar and smoothing his hair. As he reached the doorway at the front of the house he was greeted with a shout from assembled Monterey. The plaza was gay with beaming faces and bright attire. The men, women, and children of the people were on foot, a mass of color on the opposite side of the plaza: the women in gaudy cotton frocks girt with silken sashes, tawdry jewels, and spotless camisas, the coquettish reboso draping with equal grace faces old and brown, faces round and olive; the men in glazed sombreros, short calico jackets and trousers; Indians wound up in gala blankets. In the foreground, on prancing silver-trapped horses, were caballeros and donas, laughing and coquetting, looking down in triumph upon the duenas and parents who rode older and milder mustangs and shook brown knotted fingers at heedless youth. The young men had ribbons twisted in their long black hair, and silver eagles on their soft gray sombreros. Their velvet serapes were embroidered with gold; the velvet knee-breeches were laced with gold or silver cord over fine white linen; long deer-skin botas were gartered with vivid ribbon; flaunting sashes bound their slender waists, knotted over the hip. The girls and young married women wore black or white mantillas, the silken lace of Spain, regardless of the sun which might darken their

Castilian fairness. Their gowns were of flowered silk or red or yellow satin, the waist long and pointed, the skirt full; jeweled buckles of tiny slippers flashed beneath the hem. The old people were in rich dress of sober color. A few Americans were there in the ugly garb of their country, a blot on the picture.

At the door, just in front of the cavalcade, stood General Vallejo's carriage, the only one in California, sent from Sonoma for the occasion. Beside it were three superbly-trapped horses.

The governor placed the swelling nurse in the carriage, then glanced about him. "Where is Estenega?—and the Castros?" he asked.

"There are Don Jose and Dona Modeste Castro," said Chonita.

The crowd had parted suddenly, and two men and a woman rode toward the governor. One of the men was tall and dark, and his somber military attire became the stern sadness of his face. Castro was not Comandante-general of the army at that time, but his bearing was as imperious in that year of 1840 as when six years later the American Occupation closed forever the career of a man made in derision for greatness. At his right rode his wife, one of the most queenly beauties of her time, small as she was in stature. Every woman's eye turned to her at once; she was our leader of fashion, and we all copied the gowns that came to her from the city of Mexico.

But Chonita gave no heed to the Castros. She fixed her cold direct regard on the man who rode with them, and whom, she knew, must be Diego Estenega, for he was their guest. She was curious to see this enemy of her house, the political rival of her brother, the owner of the voice which had given her the first thrill of her life. He was dressed as plainly as Castro, and had none of the rich southern beauty of the caballeros. His hair was cut short like Alvarado's, and his face was thin and almost sallow. But the life that was in that face! the passion, the intelligence, the kindness, the humor, the grim determination! And what splendid vitality was in his tall thin figure, and nervous activity under the repose of his carriage! I remember I used to think in those days that Diego Estenega could conquer the world if he wished, although I suspected that he lacked one quality of the great rulers of men,— inexorable cruelty.

From the moment his horse carried him into the plaza he did not remove his eyes from Chonita's face. She lowered hers angrily after a moment. As he reached the house he sprang to the ground, and Alvarado presented the sponsors. He lifted his cap and bowed, but not as low as the caballeros who were wont to prostrate themselves before her. They murmured the usual form of salutation:

"At your feet, senorita."

"I appreciate the honor of your acquaintance."

"It is my duty and pleasure to lift you to your horse." And, still holding his cap in his hand, he led her to one of the three horses which stood beside the carriage; with little assistance she sprang to its back, and he mounted the one reserved for him.

The cavalcade started. First the carriage, then Alvarado and myself, followed by the sponsors, the Castros, the members of the Departmental Junta and their wives, then the caballeros and the donas, the old people and the Americans; the populace trudging gayly in the rear, keeping good pace with the riders, who were held in check by a fragment of

Gertrude Franklin Horn Atherton

pulp too young to be jolted.

"You never have been in Monterey before, senorita, I understand," said Estenega to Chonita. No situation could embarrass him.

"No; once they thought to send me to the convent here,—to Dona Concepcion Arguello,—but it was so far, and my mother does not like to travel. So Dona Concepcion came to us for a year, and, after, I studied with an instructor who came from Mexico to educate my brother and me." She had no intention of being communicative with Diego Estenega, but his keen reflective gaze confused her, and she took refuge in words.

"Dona Eustaquia tells me that, unlike most of our women, you have read many books. Few Californian women care for anything but to look beautiful and to marry,—not, however, being unique in that respect. Would you not rather live in our capital? You are so far away down there, and there are but few of the *gente de razon*, no?"

"We are well satisfied, senor, and we are gay when we wish. There are ten families in the town, and many rancheros within a hundred leagues. They think nothing of coming to our balls. And we have grand religious processions, and bull-fights, and races. We have beautiful canons for meriendas; and I could dance every night if I wished. We are few, but we are quite as gay and quite as happy as you in your capital." The pride of the Iturbi y Moncadas and of the Barbarina flashed in her eyes, then made way for anger under the amused glance of Estenega.

"Oh, of course," he said, teasingly. "You are to Monterey what Monterey is to the city of Mexico. But, pardon me, senorita; I would not anger you for all the gold which is said to lie like rocks under our Californias,—if it be true that certain padres hold that mighty secret. (God! how I should like to get one by the throat and throttle it out of him!) Pardon me again, senorita; I was going to say that you may be pleased to know that there is little magnificence where my ranchos are,—high on the coast, among the redwoods. I live in a house made of big ugly logs, unpainted. There are no cavalcades in the cold depths of those redwood forests, and the ocean beats against ragged cliffs. Only at Fort Ross, in her log palace, does the beautiful Russian, Princess Helene Rotscheff, strive occasionally to make herself and others forget that the forest is not the Bois of her beloved Paris, that in it the grizzly and the panther hunger for her, and that an Indian Prince, mad with love for the only fair-haired woman he has ever seen, is determined to carry her off—"

"Tell me! tell me!" cried Chonita, eagerly, forgetting her role and her enemy. "What is that? I do not know the princess, although she has sent me word many times to visit her—Did an Indian try to carry her off?"

"It happened only the other day. Prince Solano, perhaps you have heard, is chief of all the tribes of Sonoma, Valley of the Moon. He is a handsome animal, with a strong will and remarkable organizing abilities. One day I was entertaining the Rotscheffs at dinner when Solano suddenly flung the door open and strode into the room: we are old friends, and my servants do not stand on ceremony with him. As he caught sight of the princess he halted abruptly, stared at her for a moment, much as the first man may have stared at the first woman, then turned and left the house, sprang on his mustang and galloped away. The princess, you must know, is as blonde as only a Russian can be, and an extremely pretty woman, small and dainty. No wonder the mighty prince of darkness took fire. She was much amused. So was Rotscheff, and he joked her the rest of the evening. Before he left, however, I had a word with him alone, and warned him not to let the princess stray beyond the walls of the fortress. That same night I sent a courier to General Vallejo—who, fortunately, was at Sonoma—bidding him watch Solano. And, sure enough—the day I left for Monterey the Princess Helene was in hysterics, Rotscheff was swearing like a madman, and a soldier was at every carronade: word had just come from General Vallejo that he had that morning intercepted Solano in his triumphant march, at the head of six tribes, upon Fort Ross, and sent him flying back to his mountain-top in disorder and bitterness of spirit."

"That is very interesting!" cried Chonita. "I like that. What an experience those Russians have had! That terrible tragedy!—Ah, I remember, it was you who were to have aided Natalie Ivanhoff in her escape—"

"Hush!" said Estenega. "Do not speak of that. Here we are. At your service, senorita." He sprang to the whaleboned pavement in front of the little church facing the blue bay and surrounded by the gray ruins of the old Presidio, and lifted her down.

Chonita recalled, and angry with herself for having been beguiled by her enemy, took the infant from the nurse's arms and carried it fearfully up the aisle. Estenega, walking beside her, regarded her meditatively.

"What is she?" he thought, "this Californian woman with her hair of gold and her unmistakable intellect, her marble face crossed now and again by the animation of the clever American woman? What an anomaly to find on the shores of the Pacific! All I had heard of The Doomswoman, The Golden Senorita, gave me no idea of this. What a pity that our houses are at war! She is not maternal, at all events; I never saw a baby held so awkwardly. What a poise of head!

She looks better fitted for tragedy than for this little comedy of life in the Californias. A sovereignty would suit her,—were it not for her eyes. They are not quite so calm and just and inexorable as the rest of her face. She would not even make a good household tyrant, like Dona Jacoba Duncan. Unquestionably she is religious, and swaddled in all the traditions of her race; but her eyes,—they are at odds with all the rest of her. They are not lovely eyes; they lack softness and languor and tractability; their expression changes too often, and they mirror too much intelligence for loveliness, but they never will be old eyes, and they never will cease to look. And they are the eyes best worth looking into that I have ever seen. No, a sovereignty would not suit her at all; a salon might. But, like a few of us, she is some years ahead of her sphere. Glory be to the Californias—of the future, when we are dirt, and our children have found the gold!"

The baby was nearly baptized by the time he had finished his soliloquy. She had kicked alarmingly when the salt was laid on her tongue, and squalled under the deluge of water which gave her her name and also wet Chonita's sleeve. The godmother longed for the ceremony to be over; but it was more protracted than usual, owing to the importance of the restless object on the pillow in her weary arms. When the last word was said, she handed pillow and baby to the nurse with a fervent sigh of relief which made her appear girlish and natural.

After Estenega had lifted her to her horse he dried her sleeve with his handkerchief. He lingered over the task; the cavalcade and populace went on without them, and when they started they were in the rearward of the blithesome crowd.

"Do you know what I thought as I stood by you in the church?" he asked.

"No," she said, indifferently. "I hope you prayed for the fortune of the little one."

"I did not; nor did you. You were too afraid you would drop it. I was thinking how unmotherly, I had almost said unwomanly, you looked. You were made for the great world,—the restless world, where people fly faster from monotony than from a tidal wave."

She looked at him with cold dignity, but flushed a little. "I am not unwomanly, senor, although I confess I do not understand babies and do detest to sew. But if I ever marry I shall be a good wife and mother. No Spanish woman was ever otherwise, for every Spanish woman has had a good mother for example."

"You have said exactly what you should have said, voicing the inborn principles and sentiments of the Spanish woman. I should be interested to know what your individual sentiments are. But you misunderstand me. I said that you were too good for the average lot of woman. You are a woman, not a doll; an intelligence, not a bundle of shallow emotions and transient desires. You should have a larger destiny."

She gave him a swift sidelong flash from eyes that suddenly looked childish and eager.

"It is true," she said, frankly, "I have no desire to marry and have many children. My father has never said to me, 'Thou must marry;' and I have sometimes thought I would say 'No' when that time came. For the present I am contented with my books and to ride about the country on a wild horse; but perhaps—I do not know—I may not always be contented with that. Sometimes when reading Shakespeare I have imagined myself each of those women in turn. But generally, of course, I have thought little of being any one but myself.

What else could I be here?"

"Nothing; excepting a Joan of Arc when the Americans sweep down upon us. But that would be only for a day; we should be such easy prey. If I could put you to sleep and awaken you fifty years hence, when California was a modern civilization! God speed the Americans: Therein lies our only chance."

"What!" she cried. "You—you would have the Americans? You—a Californian! But you are an Estenega; that explains everything."

"I am a Californian," he said, ignoring the scorn of the last words, "but I hope I have acquired some common-sense in roving about the world. The women of California are admirable in every way,—chaste, strong of character, industrious, devoted wives and mothers, born with sufficient capacity for small pleasures. But what are our men? Idle, thriftless, unambitious, too lazy to walk across the street, but with a horse for every step, sleeping all day in a hammock, gambling and drinking all night. They are the natural followers of a race of men who came here to force fortune out of an unbroken country with little to help them but brains and will. The great effort produced great results; therefore there is nothing for their sons to do, and they luxuriously do nothing. What will the next generation be? Our women will marry Americans,—respect for men who are men will overcome prejudice,—the crossed blood will fight for a generation or two, then a race will be born worthy of California. Why are our few great men so very great to us? What have men of exceptional talent to fight down in the Californias except the barriers to its development? In England or the United States they still would be great men,—Alvarado and Castro, at least,—but they would have to work harder."

Chonita, in spite of her disapproval and her blood, looked at him with interest. His ideas and language were strikingly unlike the sentimental rhetoric of the caballeros.

"It is as you say," she admitted; "but the Californian's highest duty is loyalty to his country. Ours is a double duty, isolated as we are on this far strip of land, away from all other civilization. We should be more contemptible than Indians if we were not true to our flag."

"No wonder that you and that famous patriot of ours, Dona Eustaquia Ortega, are bonded friends. I doubt if you could hate as well as she. You have no such violence in your nature; you could neither love nor hate very hard. You would love (if you loved at all) with majesty and serenity, and hate with chili severity." While he spoke he watched her intently.

She met his gaze unflinchingly. "True, senor; I am no 'bundle of shallow emotions,' nor have I a lion in me, like Eustaquia. I am a creature of deliberation, not of impulse: I love and hate as duty dictates."

"You are by nature the most impulsive woman I ever saw," he said, much amused, "and Eustaquia's lion is a kitten to the one that sleeps in you. You have cold deliberation enough, but it is manufactured, and the result of pretty hard work at that. Like all edifices reared without a foundation, it will fall with a crash some day, and the fragments will be of very little use to you." And there the conversation ended: they had reached the plaza, and a babel of voices surrounded them. Governor Alvarado stood on the upper corridor of his house, throwing handfuls of small gold coins among the people, who were shrieking with delight. The girl guests mingled with them, seeing that no palm went home empty. Beside the governor sat Dona Martina, radiant with pride, and behind her stood the nurse, holding the infant on its pillow.

"We had better go to the house as soon as possible," said Estenega. "It is nearly time for the bull-bear fight, and we must have good seats."

They forced their way through the crowd, dismounted at the door, and went up to the corridor. The Castros and I were already there, with a number of other invited guests. The women sat in chairs, close to the corridor railing; several rows of men stood behind them.

The plaza was a jagged circle surrounded by dwelling-houses, some one story in height, others with overhanging balconies; from it radiated five streets. All corridors were crowded with the elegantly-dressed men and women of the aristocracy; large black fans were waving; every eye was flashing expectantly; the people stood on platforms which had been erected in four of the streets.

Amidst the shouts of the spectators, two vaqueros, dressed in black velvet short-clothes, dazzling linen, and stiff black sombreros, tinkling bells attached to their trappings, jingling spurs on their heels, galloped into the plaza, driving a large aggressive bull. They chased him about in a circle, swinging their reatas, dodging his onslaughts, then rode out, and four others entered, dragging an unwilling bear by a reata tied to each of its legs. By means of a long chain and much dexterity they fastened the two beasts together, freed the legs of the bear, then retired to the entrance to await events. But the bull and the bear would not fight. The latter arose on his haunches and regarded his enemy warily; the bull appeared to disdain the bear as too small game; he but lowered his horns and pawed the ground. The spectators grew impatient. The brave caballeros and dainty donas wanted blood. They tapped their feet and murmured ominously. As for the populace, it howled for slaughter. Governor Alvarado made a sign to one of the vaqueros; the man rushed abruptly upon the bull and hit him a sharp blow across the nose with the cruel quirto. The bull's dignity vanished. With the quadrupedian capacity for measuring distance, he inferred that the blow had been inflicted by the bear, who sat some twenty feet away, mildly licking his paws. He made a savage onset. The bear, with the dexterity of a vaquero, leaped aside and sprang upon the assailant's neck, his teeth meeting argumentatively in the rope-like tendons. The bull roared with pain and rage and attempted to shake him off, but he hung on; both lost their footing and rolled over and over amidst clouds of dust, a mighty noise, and enough blood to satisfy the early thirst of the beholders. Then the bull wrenched himself free; before the mountain visitor could scramble to his feet, he fixed him with his horns and tossed him on high. As the bear came down on his back with a thud and a snap which would have satisfied a bull less anxious to show what a bull could do, the victor rushed upon the corpse, kicked and stamped and bit until the blood spouted into his eyes, and pulp and dust were indistinguishable. Then how the delighted spectators clapped their hands and cried "Brava!" to the bull, who pranced about the plaza, dragging the carcass of the bear after him, his head high, his big eyes red and rolling! The women tore off their rebosos and waved them like banners, smashed their fans, and stamped their little feet; the men whirled their sombreros with supple wrists. But the bull was not satisfied; he pawed the ground with demanding hoofs; and the vaqueros galloped into the ring with another bear. Nor had they time to detach their reatas before the bull was upon the second antagonist; and they were obliged to retire in haste.

Estenega, who stood between Chonita and myself, watched The Doomswoman attentively. Her lips were compressed fiercely: for a moment they bore a strange resemblance to his own as I had seen them at times. Her nostrils were expanded, her lids half covered her eyes. "She has cruelty in her," he murmured to me as the first battle finished; "and it was her imperious wish that the bull should win, because he is the more lordly animal. She has no sympathy for the poor bundle of hair and quivering flesh that bounded on the mountain yesterday. Has she brutality in her?—just enough—"

"Brava! Brava!" The women were on their feet; even Chonita for the moment forgot herself, and beat the railing with her small fist. Another bear had been impaled and tossed and trampled. The bull, panting from his exertions, dashed about the plaza, still dragging his first victim after him. Suddenly he stopped; the blood gushed from his nostrils; he shivered like a skeleton hanging in the wind, then fell in an ignominious heap—dead.

"A warning, Diego," I said, rising and shaking my fan at him. "Be not too ambitious, else wilt thou die of thy victories. And do not love the polar star," I murmured in his ear, "lest thou set fire to it and fall to ashes thyself."

III

In the long dining-room, opening upon the large high-walled garden at the back of the Governor's house, a feast was spread for fifty people. Dona Martina sat for a little time at the head of the table, her yellow gown almost hidden by the masses of hair which her small head could not support. Castro was on one side of her, Estenega on the other, Chonita by her arch-enemy. A large bunch of artificial flowers was at each plate, and the table was loaded with yellowed chickens sitting proudly in scarlet gravy, tongues covered with walnut sauce, grilled meats, tamales, mounds of tortillas, and dulces.

Alvarado, at the lower end of the table, sat between Dona Modeste Castro and myself; and between the extremes of the board were faces glowing, beautiful, ugly, but without exception fresh and young. From all, the mantilla and serape had been removed, jewels sparkled in the lace shirts of the men, white throats were encircled by the invariable necklace of Baja Californian pearls. Chonita alone wore a string of black pearls. I never saw her without it.

Dona Martina took little part in the talk and laughter, and after a time slipped away, motioning to Chonita to take her place. The conversation turned upon war and politics, and in its course Estenega, looking from Chonita to Castro with a smile of good-natured irony said,—

"Dona Chonita is of your opinion, coronel, that California was the direct gift of heaven to the Spaniards, and that the Americans cannot have us."

Castro raised his glass to the *comadre*. "Dona Chonita has the loyal bosom of all Californian women. Our men love better the olive of peace than the flavor of discord; but did the bandoleros dare to approach our peaceful shores with dastardly intent to rob, then, thanks be to God, I know that every man among them would fight for this virgin land. Thou, too, Diego, thou wouldst unsheathe thy sword, in spite of thy pretended admiration of the Americans."

Estenega raised his shoulders. "Possibly. But in American occupation lies the hope of California. What have we done with it in our seventy years of possession? Built a few missions, which are rotting, terrorized or cajoled few thousand worthless Indians into civilized imbecility, and raised a respectable number of horses and cattle. Our hide and tallow trade is only good; the Russians have monopolized the fur trade; we continue to raise cattle and horses because it would be an exertion to suppress them; and meanwhile we dawdle away our lives very pleasurably, whilst a magnificent territory, filled with gold and richer still in soil, lies idle beneath our feet. Nature never works without a plan. She compounded a wonderful country, and she created a wonderful people to develop it. She has allowed us to drone on it for a little time, but it was not made for us; and I am sufficiently interested in California to wish to see her rise from her sleep and feel and live in every part of her." He turned suddenly to Chonita. "If I were a sculptor," he said, "I should use you as a model for a statue of California. I have the somewhat whimsical idea that you are the human embodiment of her."

Before she could muster her startled and angry faculties for reply, before Estenega had finished speaking, in fact, Castro brought his open palm down on the table, his eyes blazing.

"Oh, execrable profanation!" he cried. "Oh, unheard-of perfidy! Is it possible that a man calling himself a Californian could give utterance to such sentiments? Oh, abomination! You would invite, welcome, uphold, the American adventurer? You would tear apart the bosom of your country under pretense of doctoring its evils? You would cast this fair gift of Almighty God at the feet of American swine? Oh, Diego! Diego! This comes of the heretic books thou hast read. It is better to have heart than brain."

"True: the palpitations do not last as long. We have had proof which I need not recapitulate that to preserve California to itself it must be tied fast to Mexico, otherwise would it die of anarchy or fall a prey to the first invader. So far so good. But what has Mexico done for California? Nothing; and she will do less. She is a mother who has forgotten the child she put out to nurse. England and France and Russia would do as little. But the United States, young and ambitious, will give her greedy attention, and out of their greed will California's good be wrought. And although they sweep us from the earth, they will plant fruit where they found weeds."

Don Jose pushed back his chair violently and left the table. Estenega turned to Chonita and found her pallid, her nostrils tense, her eyes flashing.

"Traitor!" she articulated. "I hate you! And it was you— *you*—who kept my loyal brother from serving his country in the Departmental Junta. He is as full of fire and patriotism as Castro; and yet you, whose blood is ice, could be a member of the Electoral College and defeat the election of a man who is as much an honor to his country as you are a shame."

He smiled a little cruelly, but without anger or shame in his face. "Senorita," he said, "I defeated your brother because I did not believe him to be of any use to his country. He would only have been in the way as a member of the Junta, and an older man wanted the place. Your brother has Don Jose's enthusiasm without his magnetism and remarkable executive power. He is too young to have had experience, and has done neither reading nor thinking. Therefore I did my best to defeat him. Pardon my rudeness, senorita; ascribe it to revenge for calling me a traitor."

"You—you—" she stammered, then bent her head over her plate, her Spanish dignity aghast at the threatening tears. Her hand hung clinched at her side. Diego took it in spite of resistance, and, opening the rigid fingers, bent his head beneath the board and kissed them.

"I believe you are somewhat of a woman, after all," he said.

IV

The party deserted the table for the garden, there to idle until evening should give them the dance. All of the men and most of the women smoked cigaritos, the latter using the gold or silver holder, supporting it between the thumb and finger. The high walls of the garden were covered with the delicate fragrant pink Castilian roses, and the girls plucked them and laid them in their hair.

"Does it look well, Don Diego?" asked one girl, holding her head coquettishly on one side.

"It looked better on its vine," he said, absently. He was looking for Chonita, who had disappeared. "Roses are like women: they lose their subtler fragrance when plucked; but, like women, their heads always droop invitingly."

"I do not understand thee, Don Diego," said the girl, fixing her wide innocent eyes on the young man's inscrutable face. "What dost thou mean?"

"That thou art sweeter than Castilian roses," he said and passed on. "And how is, thy little one?" he asked a young matron whose lithe beauty had won his admiration a year ago, but to whom maternity had been too generous. She raised her soft brown eyes out of which the coquettish sparkle had gone.

"Beautiful! Beautiful!" she cried. "And so smart, Don Diego. He beats the air with his little fists, and—Holy Mary, I swear it!—he winks one eye when I tickle him."

Estenega sauntered down the garden endeavoring to imagine Chonita fat and classified. He could not. He paused beside a woman who did not raise her eyes at once, but coquettishly pretended to be absorbed in the conversation of those about her. She too had been married a year and more, but her figure had not lost its elegance, and she was very handsome. Her coquetry was partly fear. Estenega's power was felt alike by innocent girls and chaste matrons. There were few scandals in those days; the women of the aristocracy were virtuous by instinct and rigid social laws; but, how it would be hard to tell, Estenega had acquired the reputation of being a dangerous man. Perhaps it had followed him back from the city of Mexico, where at one time, he had spent three years as diputado, and whence returned with a brilliant and startling record of gallantry. A woman had followed on the next ship, and, unless I am much mistaken, Diego passed many uneasy hours before he persuaded her to return to Mexico. Then old Don Jose Briones' beautiful young wife was found dead in her bed one morning, and the old women who dressed the body swore that there were marks of hard skinny fingers on her throat. Estenega had made no secret of his admiration of her. At different times girls of the people had left Monterey suddenly, and vague rumors had floated down from the North that they had been seen in the redwood forests where Estenega's ranchos lay. I asked him, point-blank, one day, if these stories were true, prepared to scold him as he deserved; and he remarked coolly that stories of that sort were always exaggerated, as well as a man's success with women. But one had only to look at that face, with its expression of bitter-humorous knowledge, its combination of strength and weakness, to feel sure that there were chapters in his life that no woman outside of them would ever read. I always felt, when with Diego Estenega, that I was in the presence of a man who had little left to learn of life's phases and sensations.

"The sun will freckle thy white neck," he said to the matron who would not raise her eyes.

"Shall I bring thy mantilla, Dona Carmen?"

She looked up with a swift blush, then lowered her soft black eyes suddenly before the penetrating gaze of the man who was so different from the caballeros.

"It is not well to be too vain, senor. We must think less of those things and more of—our Church."

"True; the Church may be a surer road to heaven than a good complexion, if less of a talisman on earth. Still I doubt if a freckled Virgin would have commanded the admiration of the centuries, or even of the Holy Ghost."

"Don Diego! Don Diego!" cried a dozen horrified voices.

"Diego Estenega, if it were any man but thou," I exclaimed, "I would have thee excommunicated. Thou blasphemer! How couldst thou?"

Diego raised my threatening hand to his lips. "My dear Eustaquia, it was merely a way of saying that woman should be without blemish. And is not the Virgin the model for all women?"

"Oh," I exclaimed, impatiently, "thou canst plant an idea in people's minds, then pluck it out before their very eyes and make them believe it never was there. That is thy power,—but not over me. I know thee." We were standing apart, and I had dropped my voice. "But come and talk to me awhile. I cannot stand those babies," and I indicated with a sweep of my fan the graceful, richly-dressed caballeros whose soft drooping eyes and sensuous mouths were more promising of compliments than conversation. "Neither Alvarado nor Castro is here. Thou too wouldst have gone in a moment had I not captured thee."

"On the contrary, I should have captured you. If we were not too old friends for flirting I should say that your handsome-ugly face is the most attractive in the garden. It is a pretty picture, though," he went on, meditatively,—"those women in their gay soft gowns, coquetting demurely with the caballeros. Their eyes and mouths are like flowers; and their skins are so white, and their hair so black. The high wall, covered with green and Castilian roses, was purposely designed by Nature for them. Sometimes I have a passing regret that it is all doomed, and a half-century hence will have passed out of memory."

"What do you mean?" I asked, sharply.

"Oh, we will not discuss the question of the future. I sent Castro away from the table in a towering rage, and it is too hot to excite you. Even the impassive Doomswoman became so angry that she could not eat her dinner."

"It is your old wish for American occupation—the bando-leros! No; I will not discuss it with you: I have gone to bed with my head bursting when we have talked of it before. You might have spared poor Jose. But let us talk of something else—Chonita. What do you think of her?"

"A thousand things more than one usually thinks of a woman

after the first interview."

"But do you think her beautiful?"

"She is better than beautiful. She is original."

"I often wonder if she would be La Favorita of the South if it were not for her father's great wealth and position. The men who profess to be her slaves must have absorbed the knowledge that she has the brains they have not, although she conceals her superiority from them admirably: her pride and love of power demand that she shall be La Favorita, although her caballeros must weary her. If she made them feel their insignificance for a moment they would fly to the standard of her rival, Valencia Menendez, and her regalities would be gone forever. A few men have gone honestly wild over her, but I doubt if any one has ever really loved her. Such women receive a surfeit of admiration, but little love. If she were an unintellectual woman she would have an extraordinary power over men, with her beauty and her subtle charm; but now she is isolated. What a pity that your houses are at war!"

He had been looking away from me. As I finished speaking he turned his face slowly toward me, first the profile, which looked as if cut rapidly with a sharp knife out of ivory, then the full face, with its eyes set so deeply under the scraggy brows, its mouth grimly humorous. He looked somewhat sardonic and decidedly selfish. Well I knew what that expression meant. He had the kindest heart I had ever known, but it never interfered with a most self-indulgent nature. Many times I had begged him to be considerate of some girl who I knew charmed him for the moment only; but one secret of his success with women was his unfeigned if brief enthusiasm.

"Let her alone!" I exclaimed. "You cannot marry her. She would go into a convent before she would sacrifice the traditions of her house. And if you were not at war, and she married you, you would only make her miserably happy."

He merely smiled and continued to look me straight in the eyes.

V

I went upstairs and found Chonita reading Landor's "Imaginary Conversations." (When Chonita was eighteen,— she was now twenty-four—Don Alfredo Robinson, one of the American residents, had at her father's request sent to Boston for a library of several hundred books, a birthday gift for the ambitious daughter of the Iturbi y Moncadas. The selection was an admirable one, and a rancho would not have pleased her as well. She read English and French with ease, although she spoke both languages brokenly.) As I entered she laid down the book and clasped her hands behind her head. She looked tranquil, but less amiable than was her wont.

"Thou hast been far away from the caballeros and the donas of Monterey," I said.

"Not even among Spanish ghosts."

"I think thou carest at heart for nothing but thy books."

"And a few people, and my religion."

"But they come second, although thou wilt not acknowledge it even to thyself. Suppose thou hadst to sacrifice thy religion or thy books, never to read another? Which wouldst thou choose?"

"God of my soul! what a question! No Spanish woman was ever a truer Catholic; but to read is my happiness, the only happiness I want on earth."

"Art thou sure that to train the intellect means happiness?"

"Sure. Does it not give us the power to abstract ourselves from life when we are tired of it?"

"True, but there is another result you have not thought of. The more the intellect is developed, the more acute and aggressive is the nervous system; the more tenacious is the memory, the more has one to live with, and the higher the ideals. When the time comes for you to live you will suffer with double the intensity and depth of the woman whose nerves are dull or stunted."

"To suffer you must love, and I never shall love. Who is there to love? Books always suffice me, and I suppose there are enough in the world to make the time pass as long as I live."

I did not continue the argument, knowing the placid superiority of inexperience.

"But thou hast not yet told me which thou wouldst give up."

"The books, of course. I hope I know my duty. I would sacrifice all things to my religion. But the priests do not interfere now as they did in the last generation."

I was very religious in those days, and my heart beat with approval. "I have always said that the Church may let women read what they choose. The good principles they are born with they will adhere to."

"We are by nature conservatives, that is all. And we have need of religion. We must have something to lean on, and men are poor props, as far as I have observed. Sometimes after having read a long while in an absorbing book, particularly one that seemed to put something with a living hand into my brain and make it feel larger, I find that I am miles away from the Church; I have forgotten its existence. I always *run* back."

"*Dios!* I should think so. Yes, it is well we do need our religion. Men do not; for that reason they drop it the moment the wings on their minds grow fast—as they would, when the warm sun came out, drop the thick blanket of the Indian, borrowed and gratefully worn in dark uncertain weather. I do not dare ask Diego Estenega what he believes, lest he tell me he believes nothing and I should have to hear it. How dost thou like my friend, Chonita?"

"Art thou asking me how I like the enemy of my house? I hate him."

"If he goes to Santa Barbara with Alvarado this summer wilt thou ask him to be thy guest?"

"Of course. The enmity has always been veiled with much courtesy; and I would have him see that we know how to entertain."

I watched her covertly; I could detect no sign of interest. Presently she took up the volume of Landor and read aloud to me, the stately English sounding oddly with her Spanish accent.

VI

At ten o'clock the large sala of the Governor's house was thronged with guests, and the music of the flute, harp, and guitar floated through the open windows: the musicians sat on the corridor. How harmonious was the Monterey ballroom of that day!—the women in their white gowns of every rich material, the men in white trousers, black silk jackets, and low morocco shoes; no color except in the jewels and the rich Southern faces. The bare ugly sala, from which the uglier furniture had been removed, needed no ornaments with that moving beauty; and even the coffee-colored, high-stomached old people were picturesque. I wander through those deserted salas sometimes, and, as the tears blister my eyes, imagination and memory people the cold rooms, and I forget that the dashing caballeros and lovely donas who once called Monterey their own and made it a living picture-book are dust beneath the wild oats and thistles of the deserted cemetery on the hill. The Americans hardly know that such a people once existed.

Chonita entered the sala at eleven o'clock, looking like a snow queen. Her gold hair, which always glittered like metal, was arranged to simulate a crown; she wore a gown of Spanish lace, and no jewels but the string of black pearls. I never had seen her look so cold and so regal.

Estenega stepped out upon the corridor. "Play El Son," he said, peremptorily. Then as the vivacious music began he walked over to Chonita and clapped his hands in front of her as authoritatively as he had bidden the musicians. What he did was of frequent occurrence in the Californian ball-room, but she looked haughtily rebellious. He continued to strike his hands together, and looked down upon her with an amused smile which brought the angry color to her face. Her hesitation aroused the eagerness of the other men, and they cried loudly—

"El Son! El Son! senorita."

She could no longer refuse, and, passing Estenega with head erect, she bent it slightly to the caballeros and passed to the middle of the room, the other guests retreating to the wall. She stood for a moment, swaying her body slightly; then, raising her gown high enough for the lace to sweep the instep of her small arched feet, she tapped the floor in exact time to the music for a few moments, then glided dreamily along the sala, her willowy body falling in lovely lines, unfolding every detail of El Son, unheeding the low ripple of approval. Then, dropping her gown, she spun the length of the room like a white cloud caught in a cyclone; her garments whirred, her heels clicked, her motion grew faster and swifter, until the spectators panted for breath. Then, unmindful of the lively melody, she drifted slowly down, swaying languidly, her long round arms now lolling in the lace of her gown, now lifted to graceful sweep and curve. The caballeros shouted their appreciation, flinging gold and silver at her feet; never had El Son been given with such variations before. Never did I see greater enthusiasm until the night which culminated the tragedy of Ysabel Herrera. Estenega stood enraptured, watching every motion of her body, every expression of her face. The blood blazed in her cheeks, her eyes were like green stars and sparkled wickedly. The cold curves of her statuesque mouth were warm and soft, her chin was saucily uplifted, her heavy waving hair fell over her shoulders to her knees, a glittering veil. Where had The Doomswoman, the proud daughter of the Iturbi y Moncadas, gone?

The girls were a little frightened: this was not the Son to which they were accustomed. The young matrons frowned. The old people exclaimed, "Caramba!" "Mother of God!" "Holy Mary!" I was aghast; well as I knew her, this was a piece of audacity for which I was unprepared.

As the dance went on and she grew more and more like an untamed wood-nymph, even the caballeros became vaguely uneasy, hotly as they admired the beautiful wild thing enchaining their gaze. I looked again at Estenega and knew that his heart beat in passionate sympathy.

"I have found *her*," he murmured, exultantly. "She is California, magnificent, audacious, incomprehensible, a creature of storms and convulsions and impregnable calm; the germs of all good and all bad in her; a woman sublimated. Every husk of tradition has fallen from her."

Once, as she passed Estenega, her eyes met his. They lit with a glance of recognition, then the lids drooped and she floated on. He left the room; and when he returned she sat on a window-seat, surrounded by caballeros, as calm and as pale as when he had commanded her to dance. He did not approach her, but, joined me at the upper end of the sala, where I stood with Alvarado, the Castros, Don Thomas Larkin, the United States Consul, and a half-dozen others. We were discussing Chonita's interpretation of El Son.

"That was a strange outbreak for a Spanish girl," said Senor Larkin.

"She is Chonita Iturbi y Moncada," said Castro, severely. "She is like no other woman, and what she does is right."

The consul bowed. "True, coronel. I have seen no one here like Dona Chonita. There is a delicious uniformity about the Californian women: so reserved, shrinking yet dignified, ever on their guard. Dona Chonita changed so swiftly from the typical woman of her race to an houri, almost a bacchante,—only an extraordinary refinement of nature kept her this side of the line,—that an American would be tempted to call her eccentric."

Alvarado lifted his hand and pointed through the window to the stars. "The golden coals in the blue fire of heaven are not higher above censure," he said.

Dona Modeste raised her eyebrows. "Coals are safest when burned on the domestic hearth and carefully watched; safer still when they have fallen to ashes."

"What is this rumor of pirates on the coast?" demanded Alvarado, abruptly.

I put my hand through Estenega's arm and drew him aside. The music of the contradanza was playing, and we stood against the wall.

"Well, you know Chonita better since that dance," I said to him. "Polar stars are not unlikely to have volcanoes. Better let the deeps alone, my friend; the lava might scorch you badly. Women of complex natures are interesting studies, but dangerous to love. They wear the nerves to a point, and the tired brain and heart turn gratefully to the crystalline, idle-minded woman. She is too much like yourself, Diego. And you,—how long could you love anybody? Love with you means curiosity."

His face looked like chalk for a moment, an indication with him of suppressed and violent emotion. Then he turned his head and regarded me with a slight smile. "Not altogether. You forget that the most faithless men have been the most faithful when they have found the one woman. Curiosity and fickleness are merely parts of a restless seeking,—nothing more."

"I was sure you would acquit yourself with credit! But you have an unholy charm, and you never hesitate to exert it."

He laughed outright. "One would think I was a rattlesnake. My unholy charm consists of a reasonable amount of address born of a great weakness for women and some personal magnetism,—the latter the offspring of the habit of mental concentration—"

"And an inexorable will—"

"Perhaps. As to the exercise of it—why not? *Vive la bagatelle!*"

"It is useless to argue with you. Are you going to let that girl alone?"

"She is the only girl in the Californias whom I shall not let alone."

I could have shaken him. "To what end? And her brother? I have often wondered which would rule you in a crisis, your head or your passions."

"It would depend upon the crisis. I am afraid you are right,—that altiloquent Reinaldo will give trouble."

"Is it true that he has been conspiring with Carillo, and that an extraordinary and secret session of the Departmental Junta has been called?"

He looked down upon me with his grimmest smile. "You curious little woman! You must not put your white fingers into the Departmental pie. If you had been a man, with as good a brain as you have for a woman, you would have been an ornament to our politics. But as it is—pardon me—the better for our balancing country the less you have to do with it."

I could feel my eyes snap. "You respect no woman's mind," I said, savagely; "nothing but the woman in her. But I will not quarrel with you. Tell that baby over there to come and waltz with me."

At dawn, as we entered our room, I seized Chonita by the shoulders and shook her. "What did you mean by such a performance?" I demanded. "It was unprecedented!"

She threw back her head and laughed. "I could not help it," she said. "First I felt an irresistible desire to show Monterey that I dared do anything I chose. And then I have a wild something in me which has often threatened to break loose before; and to-night it did. It was that man. He made me."

"*Ay, Dios!*" I thought, "it has begun already."

VII

The festivities were to last a week, every one taking part but Alvarado and Dona Martina. The latter was not strong enough, the governor cared more for duty than for pleasure.

The next day we had a merienda on the hills behind the town. The green pine woods were gay with the bright colors of the young people. Here and there a caballero dashed up and down to show his horsemanship and the silver and embroidered silk of his saddle. Silver, too, were his jingling spurs, the eagles on his sombrero, the buttons on his colorous silken jacket. Horses, without exception handsomely trapped, were tethered everywhere, pawing the ground or nibbling the grass. The girls wore white or flowered silk or muslin gowns, and rebosos about their heads; the brown ugly duenas, ever at their sides, were foils they would gladly have dispensed with. The tinkle of the guitar never ceased, and the sweet voices of the girls and the rich voices of the men broke forth with the joyous spontaneity of the birds' songs about them.

Chonita wore a white silk gown, I remember flowered with blue,—large blue lilies. The reboso matched the gown. As soon as we arrived—we were a little late—she was surrounded by caballeros who hardly knew whether to like her or not, but who adhered to the knowledge that she was Chonita Iturbi y Moncada, the most famous beauty of the South.

"*Dios!* but thou art beautiful," murmured one, his dreamy eyes dwelling on her shining hair.

"*Gracias*, senor." She whispered it as bashfully as the maidens to whom he was accustomed, her eyes fixed upon a rose she held.

"Wilt thou not stay with us here in Monterey?"

She raised her eyes slowly,—he could not but feel the effort,—gave him one bewildering glance, half appealing, half protesting, then dropped them suddenly.

"Wilt thou stay with me?" panted the caballero.

"Ay, senor! thou must not speak like that. Some one will hear thee."

"I care not! God of my life! I care not! Wilt thou marry me?"

"Thou must not speak to me of marriage, senor. It is to my father thou must speak. Would I, a Californian maiden, betroth myself without his knowledge?"

"Holy heaven! I will! But give me one word that thou lovest me,—one word!"

She lifted her chin saucily and turned to another caballero, who, I doubt not, proposed also. Estenega, who had watched her, laughed.

"She acts the part to perfection," he said to me. "Either natural or acquired coquetry has more to do with saving her from the solitary plane of the intellectual woman than her beauty or her father's wealth. I am inclined to think that it is acquired. I do not believe that she is a coquette at heart, any more than that she is the marble doomswoman she fondly believes herself."

"You will tell her that," I exclaimed, angrily; "and she will end by loving you because you understand her; all women want to be understood. Why don't you go to Paris again? You have not been there for a long time."

Not deeming this suggestion worthy of answer, he left me and walked to Chonita, who was glancing over the top of her fan into the ardent eyes of a third caballero.

"You will step on a bunch of nettles in a moment," he said, practically. "Your slippers are very thin; you had better stand over here on the path." And he dexterously separated her from the other men. "Will you walk to that opening over there with me? I want to show you a better view of Monterey."

His manner had not a touch of gallantry, and she was tired of the caballeros.

"Very well," she said. "I will look at the view."

As she followed him she noted that he led her where the bushes were thinnest, and kicked the stones from her path. She also remarked the nervous energy of his thin figure. "It comes from his love of the Americans," she thought, angrily. "He must even walk like them. The Americans!" And she brought her teeth together with a sharp click.

He turned, smiling. "You look very disapproving," he said. "What have I done?"

"You look like an American! You even wear their clothes, and they are the color of smoke; and you wear no lace. How cold and uninteresting a scene would this be if all the men were dressed as you are!"

"We cannot all be made for decorative purposes. And you are as unlike those girls, in all but your dress, as I am unlike the men. I will not incur your wrath by saying that you are American: but you are modern. Our lovely compatriots were the same three hundred years ago. Will Dona California be pleased to observe that whale spouting in the bay? There is the tree beneath which Junipero Serra said his first mass in this part of the country. What a sanctimonious old fraud he must have been, if he looked anything like his pictures! Did you ever see bay bluer than that? or sand whiter? or a more perfect semicircle of hills than this? or a more straggling town? There is the Custom-house on the rocks. You will go to a ball there to-night, and hear the boom of the surf as you dance." He turned with one of his sudden impatient motions. "Suppose we ride. The air is too sharp to lie about under the trees. This white horse mates your gown. Let us go over to Carmelo."

"I should like to go," she said, doubtfully; he had made her throb with indignation once or twice, but his conversation interested her and her free spirit approved of a ride over the hills unattended by duena. "But—you know—I do not like you."

"Oh, never mind that; the ride will interest you just the same." And he lifted her to the horse, sprang on another, caught her bridle, lest she should rebel, and galloped up the road. When they were on the other side of hill he slackened speed and looked at her with a smile. She was inclined to be angry, but found herself watching the varying expressions of his mouth, which diverted her mind. It was a baffling mouth, even to experienced women, and Chonita could make nothing of it. It had neither sweetness nor softness, but she had never felt impelled to study the mouth of a caballero. And then she wondered how a man with a mouth like that could have manners so gentle.

"Are you aware," he said, abruptly, "that your brother is accused of conspiracy?"

"What?" She looked at him as if she inferred that this was the order of badinage that an Iturbi y Moncada might expect from an Estenega.

"I am not joking. It is quite true."

"It is not true! Reinaldo conspire against his government? Some one has lied. And you are ready to believe!"

"I hope some one has lied. The news is very direct, however." He looked at her speculatively. "The more obstacles the better," he thought; "and we may as well declare war on this question at once. Besides, it is no use to begin as a hypocrite, when every act would tell her what I thought of him. Moreover, he will have more or less influence over her until her eyes are opened to his true worth. She will not believe me, of course, but she is a woman who only needs an impetus to do a good deal of thinking and noting." "I am going to make you angry," he said. "I am going to tell you that I do not share your admiration of your brother. He has ten thousand words for every idea, and although, God knows, we have more time than anything else in this land of the poppy where only the horses run, still there are more profitable ways of employing it than to listen to meaningless and bombastic words. Moreover, your brother is a dangerous man. No man is so safe in seclusion as the one of large vanities and small ambitions. He is not big enough to conceive a revolution, but is ready to be the tool of any unscrupulous man who is, and, having too much egotism to follow orders, will ruin a project at the last moment by attempting to think for himself. I do not say these things to wantonly insult you, senorita, only to let you know at once how I regard your brother, that you may not accuse me of treachery or hypocrisy later."

He had expected and hoped that she would turn upon him with a burst of fury; but she had drawn herself up to her most stately height, and was looking at him with cold hauteur. Her mouth was as hard as a pink jewel, and her eyes had the glitter of ice in them.

"Senor," she said, "it seems to me that you, too, waste many words—in speaking of my brother; for what you say of him cannot interest me. I have known him for twenty-two years; you have seen him four or six times. What can you tell me of him? Not only is he my brother and the natural object of my love and devotion, but he is Reinaldo Iturbi y Moncada, the last male descendant of his house, and as such I hold him in a regard only second to that which I bear to my father. And with the blood in him he could not be otherwise than a great and good man."

Estenega looked at her with the first stab of doubt he had felt. "She is Spanish in her marrow," he thought,—"the steadfast unreasoning child of traditions. I could not well be at greater disadvantage. But she is magnificent."

"Another thing which was unnecessary," she added, "was to defend yourself to me or to tell me how you felt toward my brother, and why. We are enemies by tradition and instinct. We shall rarely meet, and shall probably never talk together again."

"We shall talk together more times than you will care to count. I have much to say to you, and you shall listen. But we will discuss the matter no further at present. Shall we gallop?"

He spurred his horse, and once more they fled through the pine woods. Before long they entered the valley of Carmelo. The mountains were massive and gloomy, the little bay was blue and quiet, the surf of the ocean roared about Point Lobos, Carmelo River crawled beneath its willows. In the middle of the valley stood the impressive yellow church, with its Roman tower and rose-window; about it were the crumbling brown hovels of the deserted Mission. Once as they rode Estenega thought he heard voices, but could not be sure, so loud was the clatter of the horses' hoofs. As they reached the square they drew rein swiftly, the horses standing upright at the sudden halt. Then strange sounds came to them through the open doors of the church: ribald shouts and loud laughter, curses and noise of smashing glass, such songs as never were sung in Carmelo before; an infernal clash of sound which mingled incongruously with the solemn mass of the surf. Chonita's eyes flashed. Even Estenega's face darkened: the traditions planted in plastic youth arose and rebelled at the desecration.

"Some drunken sailors," he said. "There—do you see that?" A craft rounded Point Lobos. "Pirates!"

"Holy Mary!" exclaimed Chonita.

"Let down your hair," he said, peremptorily; "and follow all that I suggest. We will drive them out."

She obeyed him without question, excited and interested. Then they rode to the doors and threw them wide.

The upper end of the long church was swarming with pirates; there was no mistaking those bold, cruel faces, blackened by

Gertrude Franklin Horn Atherton

sun and wind, half covered with ragged hair. They stood on the benches, they bestrode the railing, they swarmed over the altar, shouting and carousing in riotous wassail. Their coarse red shirts were flung back from hairy chests, their faces were distorted with rum and sacrilegious delight. Every station, every candlestick, had been hurled to the floor and trampled upon. The crucifix stood on its head. Sitting high on the altar, reeling and waving a communion goblet, was the drunken chief, singing a blasphemous song of the pirate seas. The voices rumbled strangely down the hollow body of the church; to perfect the scene flames should have leaped among the swinging arms and bounding forms.

"Come," said Estenega. He spurred his horse, and together they galloped down the stone pavement of the edifice. The men turned at the loud sound of horses' hoofs; but the riders were in their midst, scattering them right and left, before they realized what was happening.

The horses were brought to sudden halt. Estenega rose in his stirrups, his fine bold face looking down impassively upon the demoniacal gang who could have rent him apart, but who stood silent and startled, gazing from him to the beautiful woman, whose white gown looked part of the white horse she rode. Estenega raised his hand and pointed to Chonita.

"The Virgin," he said, in a hollow, impressive voice. "The Mother of God. She has come to defend her church. Go."

Chonita's face blanched to the lips, but she looked at the sacrilegists sternly. Fortune favored the audacity of Estenega. The sunlight, drifting through the star-window above the doors at the lower end of the church, smote the uplifted golden head of Chonita, wreathing it with a halo, gifting the face with unearthly beauty.

"Go!" repeated Estenega, "lest she weep. With every tear a heart will cease to beat."

The chief scrambled down from the altar and ran like a rat past Chonita, his swollen mouth dropping. The others crouched and followed, stumbling one over the other, their dark evil faces bloodless, their knees knocking together with superstitious terror. They fled from the church and down to the bay, and swam to their craft. Estenega and Chonita rode out. They watched the ugly vessel scurry around Point Lobos; then Chonita spoke for the first time.

"Blasphemer!" she exclaimed. "Mother of God, wilt thou ever forgive me?"

"Why not call me a Jesuit? It was a case where mind or matter must triumph. And you can confess your enforced sin, say a hundred aves or so, and be whiter than snow again; whereas, had our Mission of Carmelo been razed to the ground, as it was in a fair way to be, California would have lost an historical monument."

"And Junipero Serra's bones are there, and it was his favorite Mission," said the girl, unwillingly.

"Exactly. And now that you are reasonably sure of being forgiven, will not you forgive me? I shall ask no priest's forgiveness."

She looked at him a moment, then shook her head. "No: I cannot forgive you for having made me commit what may be a mortal sin. But, Holy Heaven!—I cannot help saying it—you are very quick!"

"For each idea is a moment born. Upon whether we wed the two or think too late depends the success or the failure of our lives."

"Suppose," she said, suddenly,—"suppose you had failed, and those men had seized me and made me captive: what then?"

"I should have killed you. Not one of them should have touched you. But I had no doubts, or I should not have made the attempt. I know the superstitious nature of sailors, especially when they are drunk. Shall we gallop back? They will have eaten all the dulces."

VIII

Monterey danced every night and all night of that week, either at Alvarado's or at the Custom-house, and every afternoon met at the races, the bull-fight, a merienda, or to climb the greased pole, catch the greased pig by its tail as it ran, or exhibit skill in horsemanship. Chonita, at times an imperious coquette, at others, indifferent, perverse, or coy, was La Favorita without appeal, and the girls alternately worshipped her—she was abstractedly kind to them—or heartily wished her back in Santa Barbara. Estenega rarely attended the socialities, being closeted with Alvarado and Castro most of the time, and when he did she avoided him if she could. The pirates had fled and were seen no more; but their abrupt retreat, as described by Chonita, continued to be an exciting topic of discussion. There were few of us who did not openly or secretly approve of Estenega's Jesuitism and admire the nimbleness of his mind. The clergy did not express itself.

On the last night of the festivities, when the women, weary with the unusually late hours of the past week, had left the ball-room early and sought their beds, and the men, being at loss for other amusement, had gone in a body to a saloon, there to drink and gamble and set fire to each other's curls and trouser-seats, the Departmental Junta met in secret session. The night was warm, the plaza deserted; all who

Gertrude Franklin Horn Atherton

were not in the saloon at the other end of the town were asleep; and after the preliminary words in Alvarado's office the Junta picked up their chairs and went forth to hold conclave where bulls and bears had fought and the large indulgent moon gave clearer light than adamantine candles. They drew close together, and, after rolling the cigarito, solemnly regarded the sky for a few moments without speaking. Their purpose was a grave one. They met to try Pio Pico for contempt of government and annoying insistence in behalf of his pet project to remove the capital from Monterey to Los Angeles; Jose Antonio Carillo and Reinaldo Iturbi y Moncada for conspiracy; and General Vallejo for evil disposition and unwarrantable comments upon the policy of the administration. None of the offenders was present.

With the exception of Alvarado, Castro, and Estenega, the members of the Junta were men of middle age, and represented the talent of California,—Jimeno, Gonzales, Arguello, Requena, Del Valle. Their dark, bearded faces, upturned to the stars, made a striking set of profiles, but the effect was marred by the silk handkerchiefs they had tied about their heads.

Alvarado spoke, finally, and, after presenting the charges in due form, continued:

"The individual enemy to the government is like the fly to the lion; it cannot harm, but it can annoy. We must brush away the fly as a vindication of our dignity, and take precaution that he does not return, even if we have to bend our heads to tie his little legs. I do not purpose to be annoyed by these blistering midgets we are met to consider, nor to have my term of administration spotted with their gall. I leave it to you, my compatriots and friends, to advise me what is best to do."

Jimeno put his feet on the side rung of Castro's chair, puffed a large gray cloud, and half closed his eyes. He then, for three-quarters of an hour, in a low, musical voice, discoursed upon the dignity of the administration and the depravity of the offenders. When his brethren were beginning to drop their heads and breathe heavily, Alvarado politely interrupted him and referred the matter to Castro.

"Imprison them!" exclaimed the impetuous General, suddenly alert. "With such a Governor and such a people, this should be a land white as the mountain-tops, unblemished by the tracks of mean ambitions and sinful revolutions. Let us be summary, although not cruel; let no man's blood flow while there are prisons in the Californias; but we must pluck up the roots of conspiracy and disquiet, lest a thousand suckers grow about them, as about the half-cut trunks of our redwood-trees, and our Californias be no better than any degenerate country of the Old World. Let us cast them into prison without further debate."

"The law, my dear Jose, gives them a trial," drawled Gonzales. And then for a half-hour he quoted such law as was known in the country. When he finished, the impatient and suppressed members of the Junta delivered their opinions simultaneously; only Estenega had nothing to say. They argued and suggested, cited evidence, defended and denounced, lashing themselves into a mighty excitement. At length they were all on their feet, gesticulating and prancing.

"Mother of God!" cried Requena. "Let us give Vallejo a taste of his own cruelty. Let us put him in a temascal and set those of his Indian victims who are still alive to roast him out—"

"No! no! Vallejo is maligned. He had no hand in that massacre. His heart is whiter than an angel's—"

"It is his liver that is white. His heart is black as a black snake's. To the devil with him!"

"Make a law that Pio Pico can never put foot out of Los Angeles again, since he loves it so well—"

"His ugly face would spoil the next generation—"

"Death to Carillo and Iturbi y Moncada! Death to all! Let the poison out of the veins of California!"

"No! no! As little blood in California as possible. Put them in prison, and keep them on frijoles and water for a year. That will cure rebellion: no chickens, no dulces, no aguardiente—"

Alvarado brought his staff of office down sharply upon a board he had provided for the purpose.

"Gentlemen," he said, "will you not sit down and smoke another cigarito? We must be calm."

The Junta took to its chairs at once. Alvarado never failed to command respect.

"Don Diego Estenega," said the Governor, "will you tell us what you have thought whilst the others have talked?"

Estenega, who had been star-gazing, turned to Alvarado, ignoring the Junta. His keen brilliant eyes gave the Governor a thrill of relief; his mouth expressed a mind made up and intolerant of argument.

"Vallejo," he said, "is like a horse that will neither run nor back into his stall: he merely stands still and kicks. His kicking makes a noise and raises a dust, but does no harm. In other words, he will irritate, but never take a responsibility.

Send him an official notice that if he does not keep quiet an armed force will march upon Sonoma and imprison him in his own house, humiliating him before the eyes of his soldiers and retainers.

"As for Pio Pico, threaten to fine and punish him. He will apologize at once and be quiet for six months, when you can call another secret session and issue another threat. It would prolong the term of his submission to order him to appear before the Junta and make it an apology with due humility.

"Now for Carillo and Reinaldo Iturbi y Moncada." He paused a moment and glanced at Chonita's grating. He had the proofs of her brother's rascality in his pocket; no one but himself had seen them. He hesitated the fraction of another moment, then smiled grimly. "Oh, Helen!" he thought, "the same old story."

"That Carillo is guilty," he said aloud, "is proven to us beyond doubt. He has incited rebellion against the government in behalf of Carlos Carillo. He is dangerous to the peace of the country. Iturbi y Moncada is young and heedless, hardly to be considered seriously; furthermore, it is impossible to obtain proof of his complicity. His intimacy with Carillo gives him the appearance of guilt. It would be well to frighten him a little by a short term of imprisonment. He is restless and easily led; a lesson in time may save his honored house from disaster. But to Carillo no quarter." He rose and stood over them. "The best thing in Machiavelli's 'Prince,'" he said, "is the author's advice to Caesar Borgia to exterminate every member of the reigning house of a conquered country, in order to avoid future revolutions and their infinitely greater number of dead. Do not let the water in your blood whimper for mercy. You are not here to protect an individual, but a country."

"You are right," said Alvarado.

The others looked at the young man who had merely given them the practical advice of statecraft as if he had opened his chest and displayed the lamp of wisdom burning. His freedom from excitement in all ordeals which animated them to madness had long ago inspired the suspicion that he was rather more than human. They uttered not a protest. Alvarado's one-eyed secretary made notes of their approval; and the Junta, after another friendly smoke, adjourned, well pleased with itself.

"Would I sacrifice my country for her a year hence?" thought Estenega, as he sauntered home. "But, after all, little harm is done. He is not worth killing, and fright and discomfort will probably cure him."

IX

Chonita and Estenega faced each other among the Castilian roses of the garden behind the Governor's house. The duena was nodding in a corner; the first-born of the Alvarados, screaming within, absorbed the attention of every member of the household, from the frantic young mother to the practical nurse.

"My brother is to be arrested, you say?"

"Yes."

"And at your suggestion?"

"Yes."

"And he may die?"

"Possibly."

"Nothing would have been done if it had not been for you?"

"Nothing."

"God of my life! Mother of God! how I hate you!"

"It is war, then?"

"I would kill you if I were not a Catholic."

"I will make you forget that you are a Catholic."

"You have made me remember it to my bitterest sorrow. I hate you so mortally that I cannot go to confession: I cannot forgive."

"I hope you will continue to hate for a time. Now listen to me. You have several reasons for hating me. My house is the enemy of yours. I am to all intents and purposes an American; you can consider me as such. I have that indifference for religious superstition and intolerance for religion's thraldom which all minds larger of circumference than a napkin-ring must come to in time. I have endangered the life of your brother, and I have opposed and shall oppose him in his political aspirations; he has my unequivocal contempt. Nevertheless, I tell you here that I should marry you were there five hundred reasons for your hatred of me instead of a paltry five. I shall take pleasure in demonstrating to you that there is a force in the universe a good deal stronger than traditions, religion, or even family ties."

His eyes were not those of a lover; they shone like steel. His mouth was forbidding. She drew back from him in terror, then struck her hands together passionately.

"I marry you!" she cried. "An Estenega! A renegade? May God cast me out of heaven if I do! There, I have sworn! I have sworn! Do you think a Catholic would break that vow? I swear it by the Church,—and I put the whole Church between us!"

"I told you just now that I would make you forget your

Church." He caught her hand and held it firmly. "A last word," he said "Your brother's life is safe: I promise you that."

"Let me go!" she said. "Let me go! I fear you." She was trembling; his warmth and magnetism had sprung to her shoulder.

He gave her back her hand. "Go," he said: "so ends the first chapter."

X

Casa Grande,[A] the mansion of the Iturbi y Moncadas in Santa Barbara, stood at the right of the Presidio, facing the channel. A mile behind, under the shadow of the gaunt rocky hills curving about the valley, was the long white Mission, with its double towers, corridor of many arches, and sloping roof covered with red tiles. Between was the wild valley where cattle grazed among the trees and the massive bowlders. The red-tiled white adobe houses of the Presidio and of the little town clustered under its wing, the brown mud huts of the Indians, were grouped in the foreground of the deep valley.

The great house of the Iturbi y Moncadas, erected in the first years of the century, was built about three sides of a court, measuring one hundred feet each way. Like most of the adobes of its time, it had but one story. A wide pillared corridor, protected by a sloping roof, faced the court, which was as bare and hard as the floor of a ball-room. Behind the dwelling were the manufactories and huts of the Indian retainers. Don Guillermo Iturbi y Moncada was the magnate of the South. His ranchos covered four hundred thousand acres; his horses and cattle were unnumbered. His Indians, carpenters, coopers, saddlers, shoemakers, weavers, manufacturers of household staples, supplied the garrison and town with the necessaries of life; he also did a large trading business in hides and tallow. Rumor had it that in the wooden tower built against the back of the house he kept gold by the bushel-basketful; but no one called him miser, for he gave the poor of the town all they ate and wore, and kept a supply of drugs for their sick. So beloved and revered was he that when earthquakes shook the town, or fires threatened it from the hills, the poor ran in a body to the court-yard of Casa Grande and besought his protection. They never passed him without saluting to the ground, nor his house without bending their heads. And yet they feared him, for he was an irascible old gentleman at times, and thumped unmercifully when in a temper. Chonita, alone, could manage him always.

When I returned to Santa Barbara with Chonita after her visit to Monterey, the yellow fruit hung in the padres' orchard, the grass was burning brown, sky and water were the hard blue of metal.

The afternoon of our arrival, Don Guillermo, Chonita, and I were on the long middle corridor of the house: in Santa Barbara one lived in the air. The old don sat on the long green bench by the sala door. His heavy, flabby, leathery face had no wrinkles but those which curved from the corners of the mouth to the chin. The thin upper lip was habitually pressed hard against the small protruding under one, the mouth ending in straight lines which seemed no part of the lips. His small slanting eyes, usually stern, could snap with anger, as they did to-day. The nose rose suddenly from the middle of his face; it might have been applied by a child sculpturing with putty; the flat bridge was crossed by erratic lines. A bang of grizzled hair escaped from the black silk handkerchief wound as tightly as a turban about his head. He wore short clothes of dark brown cloth, the jacket decorated with large silver buttons, a red damask vest, shoes of embroidered deer-skin, and a cravat of fine linen.

Chonita, in a white gown, a pale-green reboso about her shoulders, her arms crossed, her head thoughtfully bent forward, walked slowly up and down before him.

"Holy God!" cried the old man, pounding the floor with his stick. "That they have dared to arrest my son!—the son of Guillermo Iturbi y Moncada! That Alvarado, my friend and thy host, should have permitted it!"

"Do not blame Alvarado, my father. Remember, he must listen to the Departmental Junta; and this is their work." "Fool that I am!" she added to herself, "why do I not tell who alone is to blame? But I need no one to help me hate him!"

"Is it true that this Estenega of whom I hear so much is a member of the Junta?"

"It may be."

"If so, it is he, he alone, who has brought dishonor upon my house. Again they have conquered!"

"This Estenega I met—and who was *compadre* with me for the baby—is little in California, my father. If it be he who is a member of the Junta, he could hardly rule such men as Alvarado, Jimeno, and Castro. I saw no other Estenega."

"True! I must have other enemies in the North; but I had not known of it. But they shall learn of my power in the South. Don Juan de la Borrasca went to-day to Los Angeles with a bushel of gold to bail my son, and both will be with us the day after to-morrow. A curse upon Carillo—but I will speak of it no more. Tell me, my daughter,—God of my soul, but I am glad to have thee back!—what thoughtest thou of this son of the Estenegas? Is it Ramon, Esteban, or Diego? I have seen none of them since they were little ones. I remember

Diego well. He had lightning in his little tongue, and the devil in his brain. I liked him, although he was the son of my enemy; and if he had been an Iturbi y Moncada I would have made a great man of him. Ay! but he was quick. One day in Monterey, he got under my feet and I fell flat, much imperilling my dignity, for it was on Alvarado Street, and I was a member of the Territorial Deputation. I could have beaten him, I was so angry; but he scrambled to his little feet, and, helping me to mine, he said, whilst dodging my stick, 'Be not angry, senor. I gave my promise to the earth that thou shouldst kiss her, for all the world has prayed that she should not embrace thee for ninety years to come.' What could I do? I gave him a cake. Thou smilest, my daughter; but thou wilt not commend the enemy of thy house, no? Ah, well, we grow less bitter as we grow old; and although I hated his father I liked Diego. Again, I remember, I was in Monterey, and he was there; his father and I were both members of the Deputation. Caramba! what hot words passed between us! But I was thinking of Diego. I took a volume of Shakespeare from him one day. 'Thou art too young to read such books,' I said. 'A baby reading what the good priests allow not men to read. I have not read this heretic book of plays, and yet thou dost lie there on thy stomach and drink in its wickedness.' 'It is true,' he said, and how his steel eyes did flash; 'but when I am as old as you, senor, my stomach will be flat and my head will be big. Thou art the enemy of my father, but—hast thou noticed?— thy stomach is bigger than his, and he has conquered thee in speech and in politics more times than thou hast found vengeance for. Ay!—and thy ranchos have richer soil and many more cattle, but he has a library, Don Guillermo, and thou hast not.' I spanked him then and there; but I never forgot what he said, and thou hast read what thou listed. I would not that the children of Alejandro Estenega should know more than those of Guillermo Iturbi y Moncada."

"Thou hast cause to be proud of Reinaldo, for he sparkles like the spray of the fountain, and words are to him like a shower of leaves in autumn. And yet, and yet," she added, with angry candor, "he has not a brain like Diego Estenega. *He* is not a man, but a devil."

"A good brain has always a devil at the wheel; sharp eyes have sharper nerves behind; and lightning from a big soul flashes fear into a little one. Diego is not a devil,—I remember once I had a headache, and he bathed my head, and the water ran down my neck and gave me a cold which put me to bed for a week,—but he is the devil's godson, and were he not the son of my enemy I should love him. His father was cruel and vicious—but smart, Holy Mary! Diego has his brain; but he has, too, the kind heart and gentle manner—Ay! Holy God!—Come, come: here are the horses. Call Prudencia, and we will go to the bark and see what the good captain has brought to tempt us."

Four horses led by vaqueros, had entered the court-yard.

"Prudencia," called Chonita.

A door opened, and a girl of small figure, with solemn dark eyes and cream-like skin, her hair hanging in heavy braids to her feet, stepped upon the corridor, draping a pink reboso about her head.

"I am here, my cousin," she said, walking with all the dignity of the Spanish woman, despite her plump and inconsiderable person. "Thou art rested, Dona Eustaquia? Do we go to the ship, my uncle? and shall we buy this afternoon? God of my life! I wonder has he a high comb to make me look tall, and flesh-colored stockings. My own are gone with holes. I do not like white—"

"Hush thy chatter," said her uncle. "How can I tell what the captain has until I see? Come, my children."

We sprang to our saddles, Don Guillermo mounted heavily, and we cantered to the beach, followed by the ox-cart which would carry the fragile cargo home. A boat took us to the bark, which sat motionless on the placid channel. The captain greeted us with the lively welcome due to eager and frequent purchasers.

"Now, curb thy greed," cried Don Guillermo, as the girls dropped down the companion-way, "for thou hast more now than thou canst wear in five years. God of my soul! if a bark came every day they would want every shred on board. My daughter could tapestry the old house with the shawls she has."

When I reached the cabin I found the table covered with silks, satins, crepe, shawls, combs, articles of lacquer-ware, jewels, silk stockings, slippers, spangled tulle, handkerchiefs, lace, fans. The girls' eyes were sparkling. Chonita clapped her hands and ran around the table, pressing to her lips the beautiful white things she quickly segregated, running her hand eagerly over the little slippers, hanging the lace about her shoulders, twisting a rope of garnets in her yellow hair.

"Never have they been so beautiful, Eustaquia! Is it not so, my Prudencia?" she cried to the girl, who was curled on one corner of the table, gloating over the treasures she knew her uncle's generosity would make her own. "Look, how these little diamonds flash! And the embroidery on this crepe!—a dozen eyes went out ay! yi! This satin is like a tile! These fans were made in Spain! This is as big as a windmill. God of my soul!"—she threw a handful of yellow sewing-silk upon a piece of white satin; "Ana shall embroider this gown,—the golden poppies of California on a bank of

Gertrude Franklin Horn Atherton

mountain snow." She suddenly seized a case of topaz and a piece of scarlet silk and ran over to me: I being a Monterena, etiquette forbade me to purchase in Santa Barbara. "Thou must have these, my Eustaquia. They will become thee well. And wouldst thou like any of my white things? Mary! but I am selfish. Take what thou wilt, my friend."

To refuse would be to spoil her pleasure and insult her hospitality: so I accepted the topaz—of which I had six sets already—and the silk,—whose color prevailed in my wardrobe,—and told her that I detested white, which did not suit my weather-dark skin, and she was as blind and as pleased as a child.

"But come, come," she cried. "My father is not so generous when he has to wait too long."

She gathered the mass of stuff in her arms and staggered up the companion-way. I followed, leaving Prudencia raking the trove her short arms would not hold.

"Ay, my Chonita!" she wailed, "I cannot carry that big piece of pink satin and that vase. And I have only two pairs of slippers and one fan. Ay, Cho-n-i-i-ta, look at those shawls! Mother of God, suppose Valencia Menendez comes—"

"Do not weep on the silk and spoil what thou hast," called down Chonita from the top step. "Thou shalt have all thou canst wear for a year."

She reached the deck and stood panting and imperious before her father. "All! All! I must have all!" she cried. "Never have they been so fine, so rich."

"Holy Mary!" shrieked Don Guillermo. "Dost thou think I am made of doubloons, that thou wouldst buy a whole ship's cargo? Thou shalt have a quarter; no more,—not a yard!"

"I will have all!" And the stately daughter of the Iturbi y Moncadas stamped her little foot upon the deck.

"A third,—not a yard more. And diamonds! Holy Heaven! There is not gold enough in the Californias to feed the extravagance of the Senorita Dona Chonita Iturbi y Moncada."

She managed to bend her body in spite of her burden, her eyes flashing saucily above the mass of tulle which covered the rest of her face.

"And not fine raiment enough in the world to accord with the state of the only daughter of the Senor Don Guillermo Iturbi y Moncada, the delight and the pride of his old age. Wilt thou send these things to the North, to be worn by an Estenega? Thy Chonita will cry her eyes so red that she will be known as the ugly witch of Santa Barbara, and Casa Grande will be like a tomb."

"Oh, thou spoilt baby! Thou wilt have thy way—" At this moment Prudencia appeared. Nothing whatever could be seen of her small person but her feet; she looked like an exploded bale of goods. "What! what!" gasped Don Guillermo. "Thou little rat! Thou wouldst make a Christmas doll of thyself with satin that is too heavy for thy grandmother, and eke out thy dumpy inches with a train? Oh, Mother of God!" He turned to the captain, who was smoking complacently, assured of the issue. "I will let them carry these things home; but to-morrow one-half, at least, comes back." And he stamped wrathfully down the deck.

"Send the rest," said Chonita to the captain, "and thou shalt have a bag of gold to-night."

[Footnote A: In writing of Casa Grande and its inmates, no reference to the distinguished De la Guerra family of Santa Barbara is intended, beyond the description of their house and state and of the general characteristics of the founder of the family fortunes in California.]

XI

The next morning Chonita, clad in a long gown of white wool, a silver cross at her throat, her hair arranged like a coronet, sat in a large chair in the dispensary. Her father stood beside a table, parcelling drugs. The sick-poor of Santa Barbara passed them in a long line.

The Doomswoman exercised her power to heal, the birthright of the twin.

"I wonder if I can," she said to me, laying her white fingers on a knotted arm, "or if it is my father's medicines. I have no right to question this beautiful faith of my country, but I really don't see how I do it. Still, I suppose it is like many things in our religion, not for mere human beings to understand. This pleases my vanity, at least. I wonder if I shall have cause to exercise my other endowment."

"To curse?"

"Yes: I think I might do that with something more of sincerity."

The men, women, and children, native Californians and Indians, scrubbed for the occasion, filed slowly past her, and she touched all kindly and bade them be well. They regarded her with adoring eyes and bent almost to the ground.

"Perhaps they will help me out of purgatory," she said; "and it is something to be on a pedestal; I should not like to come down. It is a cheap victory, but so are most of the victories that the world knows of."

When she had touched nearly a hundred, they gathered about her, and she spoke a few words to them.

"My friends, go, and say, 'I shall be well.' Does not the Bible say that faith shall make ye whole? Cling to your faith! Believe! Believe! Else will you feel as if the world crumbled beneath your feet! And there is nothing, nothing to take its place. What folly, what presumption, to suggest that anything can—a mortal passion—" She stopped suddenly, and continued coldly, "Go, my friends; words do not come easily to me to-day. Go, and God grant that you may be well and happy."

XII

We sat in the sala the next evening, awaiting the return of the prodigal and his deliverer. The night was cool, and the doors were closed; coals burned in a roof-tile. The room, unlike most Californian salas, boasted a carpet, and the furniture was covered with green rep, instead of the usual black horsehair.

Don Guillermo patted the table gently with his open palm, accompanying the tinkle of Prudencia's guitar and her light monotonous voice. She sat on the edge of a chair, her solemn eyes fixed on a painting of Reinaldo which hung on the wall. Dona Trinidad was sewing as usual, and dressed as simply as if she looked to her daughter to maintain the state of the Iturbi y Moncadas. Above a black silk skirt she wore a black shawl, one end thrown over her shoulder. About her head was a close black silk turban, concealing, with the exception of two soft gray locks on either side of her face, what little hair she may still have possessed. Her white face was delicately cut: the lines of time indicated spiritual sweetness rather than strength.

Chonita roved between the sala and an adjoining room where four Indian girls embroidered the yellow poppies on the white satin. I was reading one of her books,—the "Vicar of Wakefield."

"Wilt thou be glad to see Reinaldo, my Prudencia?" asked Don Guillermo, as the song finished.

"Ay!" and the girl blushed.

"Thou wouldst make a good wife for Reinaldo, and it is well that he marry. It is true that he has a gay spirit and loves company, but you shall live here in this house, and if he is not a devoted husband he shall have no money to spend. It is time he became a married man and learned that life was not made for dancing and flirting; then, too, would his restless spirit get him into fewer broils. I have heard him speak twice of no other woman, excepting Valencia Menendez, and I would not have her for a daughter; and I think he loves thee."

"Sure!" said Dona Trinidad.

"That is love, I suppose," said Chonita, leaning back in her chair and forgetting the poppies. "With her a placid contented hope, with him a calm preference for a malleable woman. If he left her for another she would cry for a week, then serenely marry whom my father bade her, and forget Reinaldo in the *donas* of the bridegroom. The birds do almost as well."

Don Guillermo smiled indulgently. Prudencia did not know whether to cry or not. Dona Trinidad, who never thought of replying to her daughter, said,—

"Chonita mia, Liseta and Tomaso wish to marry, and thy father will give them the little house by the creek."

"Yes, mamacita?" said Chonita, absently: she felt no interest in the loves of the Indians.

"We have a new Father in the Mission," continued her

mother, remembering that she had not acquainted her daughter with all the important events of her absence. "And Don Rafael Guzman's son was drafted. That was a judgment for not marrying when his father bade him. For that I shall be glad to have Reinaldo marry. I would not have him go to the war to be killed."

"No," said Don Guillermo. "He must be a diputado to Mexico. I would not lose my only son in battle. I am ambitious for him; and so art thou, Chonita, for thy brother? Is it not so?"

"Yes. I have it in me to stab the heart of any man who rolls a stone in his way."

"My daughter," said Don Guillermo, with the accent of duty rather than of reproof, "thou must love without vengeance. Sustain thy brother, but harm not his enemy. I would not have thee hate even an Estenega, although I cannot love them myself. But we will not talk of the Estenegas. Dost thou realize that our Reinaldo will be with us this night? We must all go to confession to-morrow,—thy mother and myself, Eustaquia, Reinaldo, Prudencia, and thyself."

Chonita's face became rigid. "I cannot go to confession," she said. "It may be months before I can: perhaps never."

"What?"

"Can one go to confession with a hating and an unforgiving heart? Ay! that I never had gone to Monterey! At least I had the consolation of my religion before. Now I fight the darkness by myself. Do not ask me questions, for I shall not answer them. But taunt me no more with confession."

Even Don Guillermo was dumb. In all the twenty-four years

of her life she never had betrayed violence of spirit before: even her hatred of the Estenegas had been a religion rather than a personal feeling. It was the first glimpse of her soul that she had accorded them, and they were aghast. What—what had happened to this proud, reserved, careless daughter of the Iturbi y Moncadas?

Dona Trinidad drew down her mouth. Prudencia began to cry. Then, for the moment, Chonita was forgotten. Two horses galloped into the court-yard.

"Reinaldo!"

The door had but an inside knob: Don Guillermo threw it open as a young man sprang up the three steps of the corridor, followed by a little man who carefully picked his way.

"Yes, I am here, my father, my mother, my sister, my Prudencia! Ay, Eustaquia, thou too." And the pride of the house kissed each in turn, his dark eyes wandering absently about the room. He was a dashing caballero, and as handsome as any ever born in the Californias. The dust of travel had been removed—at a saloon—from his blue velvet gold-embroidered serape, which he immediately flung on the floor. His short jacket and trousers were also of dark-blue velvet, the former decorated with buttons of silver filigree, the latter laced with silver cord over spotless linen. The front of his shirt was covered with costly lace. His long botas were of soft yellow leather stamped with designs in silver and gartered with blue ribbon. The clanking spurs were of silver inlaid with gold. The sash, knotted gracefully over his hip, was of white silk. His curled black hair was tied with a blue ribbon, and clung, clustering and damp, about a low brow. He bore a strange resemblance to Chonita, in spite of the difference of color, but his eyes were merely large and brilliant: they had no stars in their shallows. His mouth was covered by a heavy silken mustache, and his profile was bold. At first glance he impressed one as a perfect type of manly strength, aggressively decided of character. It was only when he cast aside the wide sombrero—which, when worn a little back, most becomingly framed his face—that one saw the narrow, insignificant head.

For a time there was no conversation, only a series of exclamations. Chonita alone was calm, smiling a loving welcome. In the excitement of the first moments little notice was taken of the devoted bailer, who ardently regarded Chonita.

Don Juan de la Borrasca was flouting his sixties, fighting for his youth as a parent fights for its young. His withered little face wore the complacent smile of vanity; his arched brows furnished him with a supercilious expression which atoned for his lack of inches,—he was barely five feet two. His large curved nose was also a compensating gift from the godmother of dignity, and he carried himself so erectly that he looked like a toy general. His small black eyes were bright as glass beads, and his hair was ribboned as bravely as Reinaldo's. He was clad in silk attire,—red silk embroidered with butterflies. His little hands were laden with rings; carbuncles glowed in the lace of his shirt. He was moderately wealthy, but a stanch retainer of the house of Iturbi y Moncada, the devoted slave of Chonita.

She was the first to remember him, and held out her hand for him to kiss. "Thou hast the gratitude of my heart, dear friend," she said, as the little dandy curved over it. "I thank thee a thousand times for bringing my brother back to me."

"Ay, Dona Chonita, thanks be to God and Mary that I was enabled so to do. Had my mission proved unsuccessful I should have committed a crime and gone to prison with him. Never would I have returned here. Dueno adorado, ever at thy feet."

Chonita smiled kindly, but she was listening to her brother, who was now expatiating upon his wrongs to a sympathetic audience.

"Holy heaven!" he exclaimed, striding up and down the room, "that an Iturbi y Moncada, the descendant of twenty generations, should be put to shame, to disgrace and humiliation, by being cast into a common prison! That an ardent patriot, a loyal subject of Mexico, should be accused of conspiring against the judgment of an Alvarado! Carillo was my friend, and had his cause been a just one I had gone with him to the gates of death or the chair of state. But could I, *I*, conspire against a wise and great man like Juan Bautista Alvarado? No! not even if Carillo had asked me so to do. But, by the stars of heaven, he did not. I had been but the guest of his bounty for a month; and the suspicious rascals who spied upon us, the poor brains who compose the Departmental Junta, took it for granted that an Iturbi y Moncada could not be blind to Carillo's plots and plans and intrigues, that, having been the intimate of his house and table, I must perforce aid and abet whatever schemes engrossed him. Ay, more often than frequently did a dark surmise cross my mind, but I brushed it aside as one does the prompting of evil desires. I would not believe that a Carillo would plot, conspire, and rise again, after the terrible lesson he had received in 1838. Alvarado holds California to his heart; Castro, the Mars of the nineteenth century, hovers menacingly on the horizon. Who, who, in sober reason, would defy that brace of frowning gods?"

His eloquence was cut short by respiratory interference, but he continued to stride from one end of the room to the other, his face flushed with excitement. Prudencia's large eyes followed him, admiration paralyzing her tongue. Dona Trinidad smiled upward with the self-approval of the modest barn-yard lady who has raised a magnificent bantam. Don Guillermo applauded loudly. Only Chonita turned away, the truth smiting her for the first time.

"Words! words!" she thought, bitterly. "*He* would have said all that in two sentences. Is it true—*ay, triste de mi!*—what he said of my brother? I hate him, yet his brain has cut mine and wedged there. My head bows to him, even while all the Iturbi y Moncada in me arises to curse him. But my brother! my brother! he is so much younger. And if he had had the same advantages—those years in Mexico and America and Europe—would he not know as much as Diego Estenega? Oh, sure! sure!"

"My son," Don Guillermo was saying, "God be thanked that thou didst not merit thy imprisonment. I should have beaten thee with my cane and locked thee in thy room for a month hadst thou disgraced my name. But, as it happily is, thou must have compensation for unjust treatment.—Prudencia, give me thy hand."

The girl rose, trembling and blushing, but crossed the room with stately step and stood beside her uncle. Don Guillermo took her hand and placed it in Reinaldo's. "Thou shalt have her, my son," he said. "I have divined thy wishes."

Reinaldo kissed the small fingers fluttering in his, making a great flourish. He was quite ready to marry, and his pliant little cousin suited him better than any one he knew. "Day-star of my eyes!" he exclaimed, "consolation of my soul! Memories of injustice, discomfort, and sadness fall into the waters of oblivion rolling at thy feet. I see neither past nor future. The rose-hued curtain of youth and hope falls behind

Gertrude Franklin Horn Atherton

and before us."

"Yes, yes," assented Prudencia, delightedly. "My Reinaldo! my Reinaldo!"

We congratulated them severally and collectively, and, when the ceremony was over, Reinaldo cried, with even more enthusiasm than he had yet shown, "My mother, for the love of Mary give me something to eat,—tamales, salad, chicken, dulces. Don Juan and I are as empty as hides."

Dona Trinidad smiled with the pride of the Californian housewife. "It is ready, my son. Come to the dining-room, no?"

She led the way, followed by the family, Reinaldo and Prudencia lingering. As the others crossed the threshold he drew her back.

"A lump of tallow, dost thou hear, my Prudencia?" he whispered, hurriedly. "Put it under the green bench. I must have it to-night."

"Ay! Reinaldo—"

"Do not refuse, my Prudencia, if thou lovest me. Wilt thou do it?"

"Sure, my Reinaldo."

XIII

The family retired early in its brief seasons of reclusion, and at ten o'clock Casa Grande was dark and quiet. Reinaldo opened his door and listened cautiously, then stepped softly to the green bench and felt beneath for the lump of tallow. It was there. He returned to his room and swung himself from his window into the yard, about which were irregularly disposed the manufactories of the Indians, a high wall protecting the small town. All was quiet here, and had been for hours. He stole to the wooden tower and mounted a ladder, lifting it from story to story until he reached the attic under the pointed roof. Then he lit a candle, and, removing a board from the floor, peered down into the room whose door was always so securely locked. The stars shone through the uncurtained windows and were no yellower than the gold coins heaped on the large table and overflowing the baskets. Reinaldo took a long pole from a corner and applied to one end a piece of the soft tallow. He lowered the pole and pressed it firmly into the pile of gold on the table. The pole was withdrawn, and this ingenious fisherman removed a large gold fish from the bait. He fished patiently for an hour, then filled a bag he had brought for the purpose, and returned as he had come. Not to his bed, however. Once more he opened his door and stole forth, this time to the town, to hold high revel around the gaming-table, where he was welcomed hilariously by his boon companions.

Gertrude Franklin Horn Atherton

A wild fandango in a neighboring booth provided relaxation for the gamblers. In an hour or two Reinaldo found his way to this well-known haven. Black-eyed dancing-girls in short skirts of tawdry satin trimmed with cotton lace, mock jewels on their bare necks and in their coarse black hair, flew about the room and screamed with delight as Reinaldo flung gold pieces among them. The excitement continued in all its variations until morning. Men bet and lost all the gold they had brought with them, then sold horse, serape, and sombrero to the men who neither drank nor gambled, but came prepared for close and profitable bargains. Reinaldo lost his purloins, won them again, stood upon the table and spoke with torrential eloquence of his wrongs and virtues, kissed all the girls, and when by easy and rapid stages he had succeeded in converting himself into a tank of aguardiente, he was carried home and put to bed by such of his companions as were sober enough to make no noise.

XIV

Chonita, clad in a black gown, walked slowly up and down the corridor of Casa Grande. The rain should have dripped from the eaves, beaten with heavy monotony upon the hard clay of the court-yard, to accompany her mood, but it did not. The sky was blue without fleck of cloud, the sun like the open mouth of a furnace of boiling gold, the air as warm and sweet and drowsy as if it never had come in shock with human care. Prudencia sat on the green bench, drawing threads in a fine linen smock, her small face rosy with contentment.

"Why dost thou wear that black gown this beautiful morning?" she demanded, suddenly. "And why dost thou walk when thou canst sit down?"

"I had a dream last night. Dost thou believe in dreams?" She had as much regard for her cousin's opinion as for the twittering of a bird, but she felt the necessity of speech at times, and at least this child never remembered what she said.

"Sure, my Chonita. Did not I dream that the good captain would bring pink silk stockings? and are they not my own this minute?" And she thrust a diminutive foot from beneath the hem of her gown, regarding it with admiration. "And did not I dream that Tomaso and Liseta would marry? What was thy dream, my Chonita?"

"I do not know what the first part was; something very sad. All I remember is the roar of the ocean and another roar like the wind through high trees. Then a moment that shook and frightened me, but sweeter than anything I know of, so I cannot define it. Then a swift awful tragedy—I cannot recall the details of that, either. The whole dream was like a black mass of clouds, cut now and again by a scythe of lightning. But then, like a vision within a dream, I seemed to stand there and see myself, clad in a black gown, walking up and down this corridor, or one like it, up and down, up and down, never resting, never daring to rest, lest I hear the ceaseless clatter of a lonely fugitive's horse. When I awoke I was as cold as if I had received the first shock of the surf. I cannot say why I put on this black gown to-day. I make no haste to feel as I did when I wore it in that dream,—the desolation,—the endlessness; but I did."

"That was a strange dream, my Chonita," said Prudencia, threading her needle. "Thou must have eaten too many dulces for supper: didst thou?"

"No," said Chonita, shortly, "I did not."

She continued her aimless walk, wondering at her depression of spirits. All her life she had felt a certain mental loneliness, but a healthy body rarely harbors an invalid soul, and she had only to spring on a horse and gallop over the hills to feel as happy as a young animal. Moreover, the world—all the world she knew—was at her feet; nor had she ever known the novelty of an ungratified wish. Once in a while her father arose in an obdurate mood, but she had only to coax, or threaten tears,—never had she been seen to shed one,—or stamp her foot, to bring that doting parent to terms. It is true that she had had her morbid moments, an abrupt impatient desire for something that was not all light and pleasure and gold and adulation; but, being a girl of will and sense, she had turned resolutely from the troublous demands of her deeper soul, regarding them as coals fallen from a mind that burned too hotly at times.

This morning, however, she let the blue waters rise, not so much because they were stronger than her will, as because she wished to understand what was the matter with her. She was filled with a dull dislike of every one she had ever known, of every condition which had surrounded her from birth. She felt a deep disgust of placid contentment, of the mere enjoyment of sunshine and air. She recalled drearily the clock-like revolutions of the year which brought bull-fights, races, rodeos, church celebrations; her mother's anecdotes of the Indians; her father's manifold interests, ever the theme of his tongue; Reinaldo's grandiloquent accounts of his exploits and intentions; Prudencia's infinite nothings. She hated the balls of which she was La Favorita, the everlasting serenades, the whole life of pleasure which made that period of California the most perfected Arcadia the modern world has known. Some time during the past few weeks the girl had crossed her hands over her breast and lain down in her eternal tomb. The woman had arisen and come forth, blinded as yet by the light, her hands thrust out gropingly.

"It is that man," she told herself, with angry frankness. "I had not talked with him ten minutes before I felt as I do when the scene changes suddenly in one of Shakespeare's plays,—as if I had been flung like a meteor into a new world. I felt the necessity for mental alertness for the first time in my life; always, before, I had striven to conceal what I knew. The natural consequences, of course, were first the desire to feel that stimulation again and again, then to realize the littleness of everything but mental companionship. I have read that

Gertrude Franklin Horn Atherton

people who begin with hate sometimes end with love; and if I were a book woman I suppose I should in time love this man whom I now so hate, even while I admire. But I am no lump of wax in the hands of a writer of dreams. I am Chonita Iturbi y Moncada, and he is Diego Estenega. I could no more love him than could the equator kiss the poles. Only, much as I hate him, I wish I could see him again. He knows so much more than any one else. I should like to talk to him, to ask him many things. He has sworn to marry me." Her lip curled scornfully, but a sudden glow rushed over her. "Had he not been an Estenega,—yes, I could have loved him,— that calm, clear-sighted love that is born of regard; not a whirlwind and a collapse, like most love. I should like to sit with my hands in my lap and hear him talk forever. And we cannot even be friends. It is a pity."

The girl's mind was like a splendid castle only one wing of which had ever been illuminated. By the light of the books she had read, and of acute observation in a little sphere, she strove to penetrate the thick walls and carry the torch into broader halls and lofty towers. But superstition, prejudice, bitter pride, inexperience of life, conjoined their shoulders and barred the way. As Diego Estenega had discerned, under the thick Old-World shell of inherited impressions was a plastic being of all womanly possibilities. But so little did she know of herself, so futile was her struggle in the dark with only sudden flashes to blind her and distort all she saw, that with nothing to shape that moulding kernel it would shrink and wither, and in a few years she would be but a polished shell, perfect of proportion, hollow at the core.

But if strong intellectual juices sank into that sweet, pliant kernel, developing it into the perfected form of woman, establishing the current between the brain and the passions, finishing the work, or leaving it half completed, as Circumstance vouchsafed?—what then?

"Ay, Senor!" exclaimed Prudencia, as two people, mounted on horses glistening with silver, galloped into the court-yard. "Valencia and Adan!"

I came out of the sala at that moment and watched them alight: Adan, that faithful, dog-like adorer, of whose kind every beautiful woman has a half-dozen or more, Valencia the bitter-hearted rival of Chonita. She was a tall, dazzling creature, with flaming black eyes large and heavily lashed, and a figure so lithe that she seemed to sweep downward from her horse rather than spring to the ground. She had the dark rich skin of Mexico—another source of envy and hatred, for the Iturbi y Moncadas, like most of the aristocracy of the country, were of pure Castilian blood and as white as porcelain in consequence—and a red full mouth.

"Welcome, my Chonita!" she cried. "*Valgame Dios!* but I am glad to see thee back!" She kissed Chonita effusively. "Ay, my poor brother!" she whispered, hurriedly. "Tell him that thou art glad to see him." And then she welcomed me with words that fell as softly as rose-leaves in a zephyr, and patted Prudencia's head.

Chonita, with a faint flush on her cheek, gave Adan her hand to kiss. She had given this faithful suitor little encouragement, but his unswerving and honest devotion had wrung from her a sort of careless affection; and she told me that first night in Monterey that if she ever made up her mind to marry she thought she would select Adan: he was more tolerable than any one she knew. It is doubtful if he had crossed her mind since; and now, with all a woman's unreason, she conceived a sudden and violent dislike for him because she had treated him too kindly in her thoughts. I liked Adan Menendez; there was something manly and sure about him,—the latter a restful if not a fascinating quality. And I liked his appearance. His clear brown eyes had a kind direct regard. His chin was round, and his profile a little thick; but the gray hair brushed up and away from his low forehead gave dignity to his face. His figure was pervaded with the indolence of the Californian.

"At your feet, senorita mia," he murmured, his voice trembling.

"It gives me pleasure to see thee again, Adan. Hast thou been well and happy since I left?"

It was a careless question, and he looked at her reproachfully.

"I have been well, Chonita," he said.

At this moment our attention was startled by a sharp exclamation from Valencia. Prudencia had announced her engagement. Valencia had refused many suitors, but she had intended to marry Reinaldo Iturbi y Moncada. Not that she loved him: he was the most brilliant match in three hundred leagues. Within the last year he had bent the knee to the famous coquette; but she had lost her temper one day,—or, rather, it had found her,—and after a violent quarrel he had galloped away, and gone almost immediately to Los Angeles, there to remain until Don Juan went after him with a bushel of gold. She controlled herself in a moment, and swayed her graceful body over Prudencia, kissing her lightly on the cheek.

"Thou baby, to marry!" she said, softly. "Thou didst take away my breath. Thou dost look no more than fourteen years. I had forgotten the grand merienda of thy eighteenth birthday."

Prudencia's little bosom swelled with pride at the discomfiture of the haughty beauty who had rarely remembered to notice her. Prudencia was not poor; she owned a goodly rancho; but it was an hacienda to the state of a Menendez.

"Thou wilt be one of my bridesmaids, no, Dona Valencia?" she asked.

"That will be the proud day of my life," said Valencia, graciously.

"We have a ball to-night," said Chonita.

"Thou wouldst have had word to-day. Thou wilt stay now, no? and not ride those five leagues twice again? I will send for thy gown."

"Truly, I will stay, my Chonita. And thou wilt tell me all about thy visit to Monterey, no?"

"All? Ay! sure!"

Adan kissed both Prudencia's little hands in earnest congratulation. As he did so, the door of Reinaldo's room opened, and the heir of the Iturbi y Moncadas stepped forth, gorgeous in black silk embroidered with gold. He had slept off the effects of the night's debauch, and cold water had restored his freshness. He kissed Prudencia's hand, his own to us, then bent over Valencia's with exaggerated homage.

"At thy feet, O loveliest of California's daughters. In the immensity of thought, going to and coming from Los Angeles, my imagination has spread its wings like an eagle. Thou hast been a beautiful day-dream, posing or reclining, dancing, or swaying with grace superlative on thy restive steed. I have not greeted my good friend Adan. I can but look and look and keep on looking at his incomparable sister, the rose of roses, the queen of queens."

"Thy tongue carols as easily as a lark's," said Valencia, with but half-concealed bitterness. "Thou couldst sing all day,— and the next forget."

"I forget nothing, beautiful senorita,—neither the fair days of spring nor the ugly storms of winter. And I love the sunshine and flee from the tempest. Adan, brother of my heart, welcome as ever to Casa Grande—Ay! here is my father. He looks like Sancho Panza."

Don Guillermo's sturdy little mustang bore him into the court-yard, shaking his stout master not a little. The old gentleman's black silk handkerchief had fallen to his shoulders: his face was red, but covered with a broad smile.

"I have letters from Monterey," he said, as Reinaldo and Adan ran down the steps to help him alight. "Alvarado goes by sea to Los Angeles this month, but returns by land in the next, and will honor us with a visit of a week. I shall write to him to arrive in time for the wedding. Several members of the Junta come with him,—and of their number is Diego Estenega."

"Who?" cried Reinaldo. "An Estenega? Thou wilt not ask him to cross the threshold of Casa Grande?"

"I always liked Diego," said the old man, somewhat confusedly. "And he is the friend of Alvarado. How can I avoid to ask him, when he is of the party?"

"Let him come," cried Reinaldo. "God of my life!—I am glad that he comes, this lord of redwood forests and fog-bound cliffs. It is well that he see the splendor of the Iturbi y Moncadas,—our pageants and our gay diversions, our cavalcades of beauty and elegance under a canopy of smiling blue. Glad I am that he comes. Once for all shall he learn that, although his accursed family has beaten ours in war and politics, he can never hope to rival our pomp and state."

"Ah!" said Valencia to Chonita, "I have heard of this Diego Estenega. I too am glad that he comes. I have the advantage of thee this time, my friend. Thou and he must hate each other, and for once I am without a rival. He shall be my slave." And she tossed her spirited head.

"He shall not!" cried Chonita, then checked herself abruptly, the blood rushing to her hair. "I hate him so," she continued hurriedly to the astonished Valencia, "that I would see no woman show him favor. Thou wilt not like him, Valencia. He is not handsome at all,—no color in his skin, not even white, and eyes in the back of his head. No mustache, no curls, and a mouth that looks,—oh, that mouth, so grim, so hard!—no, it is not to be described. No one could; it makes you hate him. And he has no respect for women; he thinks they were made to please the eye, no more. I do not think he would look ten seconds at an ugly woman. Thou wilt not like him, Valencia, sure."

"Ay, but I think I shall. What thou hast said makes me wish to see him the more. God of my life! but he must be different from the men of the South. And I shall like that."

"Perhaps," said Chonita, coldly. "At least he will not break thy heart, for no woman could love him. But come and take thy siesta, no? and refresh thyself for the dance. I will send thee a cup of chocolate." And, bending her head to Adan, she swept down the corridor, followed by Valencia.

XV

Those were two busy months before Prudencia's wedding.
Twenty girls, sharply watched and directed by Dona Trinidad
and the sometime mistress of Casa Grande, worked upon the
marriage wardrobe. Prudencia would have no use for more
house-linen; but enough fine linen was made into underclothes
to last her a lifetime. Five keen-eyed girls did nothing but
draw the threads for deshalados, and so elaborate was the
open-work that the wonder was the bride did not have bands
and stripes of rheumatism. Others fashioned crepes and
flowered silks and heavy satins into gowns with long pointed
waists and full flowing skirts, some with sleeves of lace and
high to the base of the throat, others cut to display the plump
whiteness of the owner. Twelve rebosos were made for her;
Dona Trinidad gave her one of her finest mantillas; Chonita,
the white satin embroidered with poppies, for which she had
conceived a capricious dislike. She also invited Prudencia to
take what she pleased from her wardrobe; and Prudencia, who
was nothing if not practical, helped herself to three gowns
which had been made for Chonita at great expense in the city
of Mexico, four shawls of Chinese crepe, a roll of pineapple
silk, and an American hat.

The house until within two weeks of the wedding was full of
visitors,—neighbors whose ranchos lay ten leagues away or
nearer, and the people of the town; all of them come to offer

congratulations, chatter on the corridor by day and dance in the sala by night. The court was never free of prancing horses pawing the ground for eighteen hours at a time under their heavy saddles. Dona Trinidad's cooking-girls were as thick in the kitchen as ants on an anthill, for the good things of Casa Grande were as famous as its hospitality, and not the least of the attractions to the merry visitors. When we did not dance at home we danced at the neighbors' or at the Presidio. During the last two weeks, however, every one went home to rest and prepare for the festivities to succeed the wedding; and the old house was as quiet as a canon in the mountains.

Chonita took a lively concern in the preparations at first, but her interest soon evaporated, and she spent more and more time in the little library adjoining her bedroom. She did less reading than thinking, however. Once she came to me and tried for fifteen minutes to draw from me something in Estenega's dispraise; and when I finally admitted that he had a fault or two I thought she would scalp me. Still, at this time she was hardly more than fascinated, interested, tantalized by a mind she could appreciate but not understand. If they had never met again he would gradually have moved backward to the horizon of her memory, growing dim and more dim, hovered in a cloud-bank for a while, then disappeared into that limbo which must exist somewhere for discarded impressions, and all would have been well.

XVI

The evening before the wedding Prudencia covered her demure self with black gown and reboso, and, accompanied by Chonita, went to the Mission to make her last maiden confession. Chonita did not go with her into the church, but paced up and down the long corridor of the wing, gazing absently upon the deep wild valley and peaceful ocean, seeing little beyond the images in her own mind.

That morning Alvarado and several members of the Junta had arrived, but not Estenega. He had come as far as the Rancho Temblor, Alvarado explained, and there, meeting some old friends, had decided to remain over night and accompany them the next day to the ceremony. As Chonita had stood on the corridor and watched the approach of the Governor's cavalcade her heart had beaten violently, and she had angrily acknowledged that her nervousness was due to the fact that she was about to meet Diego Estenega again. When she discovered that he was not of the party, she turned to me with pique, resentment, and disappointment in her face.

"Even if I cannot ever like him," she said, "at least I might have the pleasure of hearing him talk. There is no harm in that, even if he is an Estenega, a renegade, and the enemy of my brother. I can hate him with my heart and like him with my mind. And he must have cared little to see us again, that he could linger for another day."

"I am mad to see Don Diego Estenega," said Valencia, her red lips pouting. "Why did he, of all others, tarry?"

"He is fickle and perverse," I said,—"the most uncertain man I know."

"Perhaps he thought to make us wish to see him the more," suggested Valencia.

"No," I said: "he has no ridiculous vanities."

Chonita wandered back and forth behind the arches, waiting for Prudencia's long confession of sinless errors to conclude.

"What has a baby like that to confess?" she thought, impatiently. "She could not sin if she tried. She knows nothing of the dark storms of rage and hatred and revenge which can gather in the breasts of stronger and weaker beings. I never knew, either, until lately; but the storm is so black I dare not face it and carry it to the priest. I am a sort of human chaos, and I wish I were dead. I thought to forget him, and I see him as plainly as on that morning when he told me that it was he who would send my brother to prison—"

She stopped short with a little cry. Diego Estenega stood before the Mission in the broad swath of moonlight. She had heard a horse gallop up the valley, but had paid no attention to the familiar sound. Estenega had appeared as suddenly as if he had arisen from the earth.

"It is I, senorita." He ascended the Mission steps. "Do not fear. May I kiss your hand?"

She gave him her hand, but withdrew it hurriedly. Of the tremendous mystery of sex she knew almost nothing. Girls were brought up in such ignorance in those days that many a bride ran home to her mother on her wedding night; and books teach Innocence little. But she was fully conscious that there was something in the touch of Estenega's lips and hand that startled while it thrilled and enthralled.

"I thought you stayed with the Ortegas to-night," she said. Oh, blessed conventions!

"I did,—for a few hours. Then I wanted to see you, and I left them and came on. At Casa Grande I found no one but Eustaquia; every one else had gone to the gardens; and she told me that you were here."

Chonita's heart was beating as fast as it had beaten that morning; even her hands shook a little. A glad wave of warmth rushed over her. She turned to him impetuously. "Tell me?" she exclaimed. "Why do I feel like this for you? I hate you: you know that. There are many reasons,—five; you counted them. And yet I feel excited, almost glad, at your coming. This morning I was disappointed when you did not. Tell me,—you know everything, and I so little,—why is it?"

Her cheeks were flushed, her eyes terrified and appealing. She looked very lovely and natural. Probably for the first time in his life Estenega resisted a temptation. He passionately wished to take her in his arms and tell her the truth. But he was too clever a man; there was too much at stake; if he frightened her now he might never even see her again. Moreover, she appealed to his chivalry. And it suddenly occurred to him that so sweet a heart would be warped in its waking if passion bewildered and controlled her first.

"Dona Chonita," he said, "like all women,—all beautiful and spoiled women,—you demand variety. I happen to be made of harder stuff than your caballeros, and you have not seen me for two months; that is all."

"And if I saw you every day for two months would I no longer care whether you came or went?"

"Undoubtedly.

"Is it sweet or terrible to feel this way?" thought the girl. "Would I regret if he no longer made me tremble, or would I go on my knees and thank the Blessed Virgin?" Aloud she said, "It was strange for me to ask you such questions; but it is as if you had something in your mind separate from yourself, and that *it* would tell me, and you could not prevent its being truthful. I do not believe in *you*; you look as if nothing were worth the while to lie or tell the truth about; but your mind is quite different. It seems to me that it knows all things, that it is as cold and clear as ice."

"What a whimsical creature you are! My mind, like myself,—I feel as if I were twins,—is at your service. Forget that I am Diego Estenega. Regard me as a sort of archive of impressions which may amuse or serve you as the poorest of your books do. That they happen to be catalogued under the general title of Diego Estenega is a mere detail; an accident, for that matter; they might be pigeon-holed in the skull of a Bandini or a Pico. I happen to be the magnet, that is all."

"If I could forget that you were an Estenega,—just for a week, while you are here," she said, wistfully.

"You are a woman of will and imagination,—also of variety. Make an experiment; it will interest you. Of course there will be times when you will be bitterly conscious that I am the enemy of your house; it would be idle to expect otherwise; but when we happen to be apart from disturbing influences, let us agree to forget that we are anything but two human beings, deeply congenial. As for what I said in the garden at Monterey, the last time we spoke together,—I shall not bother you."

"You no longer care?" she exclaimed.

"I did not say that. I said I should not bother you,— recognizing your hostility and your reasons. Be faithful to your traditions, my beautiful doomswoman. No man is worth the sacrifice of those dear old comrades. What presumption for a man to require you to abandon the cause of your house, give up your brother, sacrifice one or more of your religious principles; one, too, who would open his doors to the Americans you hate! No man is worth such a sacrifice as that."

"No," she said, "no man." But she said it without enthusiasm.

"A man is but one; traditions are fivefold, and multiplied by duty. Poor grain of sand—what can he give, comparable to the cold serene happiness of fidelity to self? Love is sweet,— horribly sweet,—but so common a madness can give but a tithe of the satisfaction of duty to pure and lofty ideals."

"I do not believe that." The woman in her arose in resentment. "A life of duty must be empty, cold, and wrong. It was not that we were made for."

"Let us talk little of love, senorita: it is a dangerous subject."

"But it interests me, and I should like to understand it."

"I will explain the subject to you fully, some day. I have a fancy to do that on my own territory,—up in the redwoods—"

"Here is Prudencia."

A small black figure swept down the steps of the church. She bowed low to Estenega when he was presented, but uttered no word. The Indian servants brought the horses to the door, and they rode down the valley to Casa Grande.

XVII

The guests of Casa Grande—there were many besides Alvarado and his party; the house was full again—were gathered with the family on the corridor as Estenega, Chonita, and Prudencia dismounted at the extreme end of the court-yard. As Reinaldo saw the enemy of his house approach he ran down the steps, advanced rapidly, and bowed low before him.

"Welcome, Senor Don Diego Estenega," he said,—"welcome to Casa Grande. The house is thine. Burn it if thou wilt. The servants are thine; I myself am thy servant. This is the supreme moment of my life, supremer even than when I learned of my acquittal of the foul charges laid to my door by scheming and jealous enemies. It is long—alas!—since an Estenega and an Iturbi y Moncada have met in the court-yard of the one or the other. Let this moment be the seal of peace, the death of feud, the unification of the North and the South."

"You have the hospitality of the true Californian, Don Reinaldo. It gives me pleasure to accept it."

"Would, then, thy pleasure could equal mine!" "Curse him!" he added to Chonita, as Estenega went up the steps to greet Don Guillermo and Dona Trinidad, "I have just received positive information that it was he who kept me from distinguishing myself and my house in the Departmental Junta, he who cast me in a dungeon. It poisons my happiness to sleep under the same roof with him."

"Ay!" exclaimed Chonita. "Why canst thou not be more sincere, my brother? Hospitality did not compel thee to say so much to thine enemy. Couldst thou not have spoken a few simple words like himself, and not blackened thy soul?"

"My sister! thou never spokest to me so harshly before. And on my marriage eve!"

"Forgive me, my most beloved brother. Thou knowest I love thee. But it grieves me to think that even hospitality could make thee false."

When they ascended the steps, not a woman was to be seen; all had followed Prudencia to her chamber to see the *donas* of the groom, which had arrived that day from Mexico. Chonita tarried long enough to see that her father had forgotten the family grievance in his revived susceptibility to Estenega, then went to Prudencia's room. There women, young and old, crowded each other, jabbering like monkeys. The little iron bed, the chairs and tables, every article of furniture, in fact, but the altar in the corner, displayed to advantage exquisite materials for gowns, a mass of elaborate underclothing, a white lace mantilla to be worn at the bridal, lace flounces fine and deep, crepe shawls, sashes from Rome, silk stockings by the dozen. On a large table were the more delicate and valuable gifts: a rosary of topaz, the cross a fine piece of carving; a jeweled comb; a string of pearls; diamond hoops for the ears; a large pin painted with a head of Guadalupe, the patron saint of California; and several fragile fans. Quite apart, on a little table, was the crown and pride of the *donas*,—six white cobweb-like smocks, embroidered, hemistitched, and deshaladoed. Did any

Californian bridegroom forget that dainty item he would be repudiated on his wedding-eve.

"God of my life!" murmured Valencia, "he has taste as well as gold. And all to go on that round white doll!"

There was little envy among the other girls. Their eyes sparkled with good-nature as they kissed Prudencia and congratulated her. The older women patted the things approvingly; and, between religion, a *donas* to satisfy an angel, and prospective bliss, Prudencia was the happiest little bride-elect in all The Californias.

"Never were such smocks!" cried one of the girls. "Ay! he will make a good husband. That sign never fails."

"Thou must wear long, long trains now, my Prudencia, and be as stately as Chonita."

"Ay!" exclaimed Prudencia. Did not every gown already made have a train longer than herself?

"Thou needst never wear a mended stocking with all these to last thee for years," said another: never had silk stockings been brought to the Californias in sufficient plenty for the dancing feet of its daughters.

"I shall always mend my stockings," said Prudencia, "I myself."

"Yes," said one of the older women, "thou wilt be a good wife and waste nothing."

Valencia laid her arm about Chonita's waist. "I wish to meet Don Diego Estenega," she said. "Wilt thou not present him to me?"

"Thou art very forward," said Chonita, coldly. "Canst thou not wait until he comes thy way?"

"No, my Chonita; I wish to meet him now. My curiosity devours me."

"Very well; come with me and thou shalt know him.—Wilt thou come too, Eustaquia? There are only men on the corridor."

We found Diego and Don Guillermo talking politics in a corner, both deeply interested. Estenega rose at once.

"Don Diego Estenega," said Chonita, "I would present you to the Senorita Dona Valencia Menendez, of the Rancho del Fuego."

Estenega bowed. "I have heard much of Dona Valencia, and am delighted to meet her."

Valencia was nonplussed for a moment; he had not given her the customary salutation, and she could hardly murmur the customary reply. She merely smiled and looked so handsome that she could afford to dispense with words.

"A superb type," said Estenega to me, as Don Guillermo claimed the beauty's attention for a moment. "But only a type; nothing distinctive."

Nevertheless, ten minutes later, Valencia, with the manoeuvring of the general of many a battle, had guided him to a seat in the sala under Dona Trinidad's sleepy wing, and her eyes were flashing the language of Spain to his. I saw Chonita watch them for a moment, in mingled surprise and doubt, then saw a sudden look of fear spring to her eyes as she turned hastily and walked away.

Again I shared her room,—the thirty rooms and many in the out-buildings were overflowing with guests who had come a hundred leagues or less,—and after we had been in bed a half-hour, Chonita, overcome by the insinuating power of that time-honored confessional, told me of her meeting with Estenega at the Mission. I made few comments, but sighed; I knew him so well. "It will be strange to even seem to be friends with him," she added,—"to hate him in my heart and yet delight to talk with him, and perhaps to regret when he leaves."

"Are you sure that you still hate him?"

She sat up in bed. The solid wooden shutters were closed, but over the door was a small square aperture, and through this a stray moonbeam drifted and fell on her. Her hair was tumbling about her shoulders, and she looked decidedly less statuesque than usual.

"Eustaquia," she said, solemnly, "I believe I can go to confession."

XVIII

At sunrise the next morning the guests of Casa Grande were horsed and ready to start for the Mission. The valley between the house and the Mission was alive with the immediate rancheros and their families, and the people of the town, aristocrats and populace.

At Estenega's suggestion, I climbed with him to the attic of the tower, much to the detriment of my frock. But I made no complaint after Diego had removed the dusty little windows on both sides and I looked through the apertures at the charming scene. The rising sun gave added fire to the bright red tiles of the long white Mission, and threw a pink glow on its noble arches and towers and on the white massive aqueduct. The bells were crashing their welcome to the bride. The deep valley, wooded and rocky, was pervaded by the soft glow of the awakening, but was as lively as midday. There were horses of every color the Lord has decreed that horses shall wear. The saddles upon them were of embossed leather or rich embroidered silk heavily mounted with silver. Above all this gorgeousness sat the caballeros and the donas, in velvet and silk, gold lace and Spanish, jewels and mantillas, and silver-weighted sombreros; a confused mass of color and motion; a living picture, shifting like a kaleidoscope. Nor was this all: brown, soberly-dressed old men and women in satin-padded carretas,—heavy ox-carts

Gertrude Franklin Horn Atherton

on wheels made from solid sections of trees, and driven by a ganan seated on one of the animals; the populace in cheap finery, some on foot, others astride old mules or broken-winded horses, two or three on one lame old hack; all chattering, shouting, eager, interested, impatiently awaiting the bride and a week of pleasure.

In the court-yard and plaza before it the guests of the house were mounted on a caponera of palominas,—horses peculiar to the country; beautiful creatures, golden-bronze, and burnished, with luxuriant manes and tails which waved and shone like the sparkling silver of a water-fall. A number were riderless, awaiting the pleasure of the bridal party. One alone was white as a Californian fog. He lifted his head and pranced as if aware of his proud distinction. The aquera and saddle which embellished his graceful beauty were of pink silk worked with delicate leaves in gold and silver thread. The stirrups, cut from blocks of wood, were elaborately carved. The glistening reins were made from the long crystal hairs of his mane, and linked with silver. A strip of pink silk, joined at the ends with a huge rosette, was hung from the high silver pommel of the saddle, depending on the left side,—a stirrup for my lady's foot.

A deeper murmur, a sudden lining of sombreros and waving of little hands, proclaimed that the bridal party had appeared, and we hastened down.

Prudencia, the mantilla of the *donas* depending from a comb six inches high, was attired in a white satin gown with a train of portentous length, and looked like a kitten with a long tail. Reinaldo was dazzling. He wore white velvet embroidered with gold; his linen and lace were more fragile than cobwebs; his white satin slippers were clasped with diamond buckles, the same in which his father had married; his jacket was buttoned with diamonds. His white velvet sombrero was covered with plumes. Never have I seen so splendid a bride-groom. I saw Estenega grin; but I maintain that, whatever Reinaldo's deficiencies, he was a picture to be thankful for that morning.

Dona Trinadad was quietly gowned in gray satin, but Don Guillermo was as picturesque in his way as his son. His black silk handkerchief had been knotted hurriedly about his head, and the four corners hung upon his neck. His short breeches were of red velvet, his jacket of blue cloth trimmed with large silver buttons and gold lace; his vest was of yellow damask, his linen embroidered. Attached to his slippers were enormous silver spurs inlaid with gold, the rowels so long that they scratched more trains than one that day.

The bridesmaids stood in a group apart, a large bouquet: each wore a gown of a different color. Valencia blazed forth in yellow, and flashed triumphant glances at Estenega, now and again one of irrepressible envy and resentment at Reinaldo. Chonita looked like a water-witch in pale green covered with lace that stirred with every breath of air; her mantilla was as delicate as sea-spray. About her was something subtle, awakened, restive, that I noticed for the first time. Once she intercepted one of Valencia's lavish glances, and her own eyes were extremely wicked and dangerous for a moment. I looked at Estenega. He was regarding her with a fierce intensity which made him oblivious for the moment of his surroundings. I looked at Valencia. Thunderclouds were those heavy brows, lowered to the lightning which sprang from depths below. I looked again at Chonita. The pink color was in her marble face; pinker were her carven lips.

"God of my soul!" I said to Estenega. "Go home."

"My Prudencia," said Don Guillermo. He lifted her to the pink saddle, adjusted her foot in the pink ribbon, climbed up behind her, placed one arm about her waist, took the bridle in his other hand, and cantered out of the court-yard. Reinaldo sprang to his horse, lifted his mother in front of him, and followed. Then went the bridesmaids; and the rest of us fell into line as we listed. As we rode up the valley, those awaiting us joined the cavalcade, the populace closing it, spreading out like a fan attached to the tail of a snake. The bells rang out a joyful discordant peal; the long undulating line of many colors wound through the trees, passed the long corridor of the Mission, to the stone steps of the church.

The ceremony was a long one, for communion was given the bride and groom; and during the greater part of it I do not think Estenega removed his gaze from Chonita. I could not help observing her too, although I was deeply impressed with the solemnity of the occasion. Her round womanly figure had never appeared to greater advantage than in that close-fitting gown; her hips being rather wide, she wore fewer gathers than was the fashion. Her faultless arms had a warmth in their whiteness; the filmy lace of her mantilla caressed a throat so full and round and white and firm that it seemed to invite other caresses; even the black pearls clung lovingly about it. Her graceful head was bent forward a little, and the soft black lashes brushed her cheeks. The pink flush was still in her face, like the first tinge of color on the chill desolation of dawn.

"Is she not beautiful?" whispered Estenega, eagerly. "Is not that a woman to make known to herself? Think of the infinite possibilities, the sublimation of every—"

Here I ordered him to keep quiet, reminding him that he was in church, a fact he had quite forgotten. I inferred that he remembered it later, for he moved restlessly more than once and looked longingly toward the door.

It was over at last, and as the bride and groom appeared in the door of the church and descended the steps, a salute was fired from the Presidio. On the long corridor a table had been built from end to end and a goodly banquet provided by the padres. We took our seats at once, the populace gathering about a feast spread for them on the grass.

Padre Jimeno, the priest who had officiated at the ceremony, sat at the head of the table; the other priests were scattered among us, and good company all of them were. We were a very lively party. Prudencia was toasted until her calm important head whirled. Reinaldo made a speech as full of flowers as the occasion demanded. Alvarado made one also, five sentences of plain well-chosen words, to which the bridegroom listened with scorn. Now and again a girl swept the strings of a guitar or a caballero sang. The delighted shrieks of the people came over to us; at regular intervals cannons were fired.

Estenega found himself seated between Chonita and Valencia. I was opposite, and beginning to feel profoundly fascinated by this drama developing before my eyes. I saw that he was amused by the situation and not in the least disconcerted. Valencia was nervous and eager. Chonita, whose pride never failed her, had drawn herself up and looked coldly indifferent.

"Senor," murmured Valencia, "thou wilt tarry with us long, no? We have much to show thee in Santa Barbara, and on our ranchos."

"I fear that I can stay but a week, senorita. I must return to Los Angeles."

"Would nothing tempt thee to stay, Don Diego?"

He looked into her rich Southern face and approved of it: when had he ever failed to approve of a pretty woman? "Thine eyes, senorita, would tempt a man to forget more than duty."

"And thou wilt stay?"

"When I leave Santa Barbara what I take of myself will not be worth leaving."

"Ay! and what thou leavest thou never shalt have again."

"There is my hope of heaven, senorita."

He turned from this glittering conversation to Chonita.

"You are a little tired," he said, in a low voice. "Your color has gone, and the shadows are coming about your eyes."

The suspicion was borne home to her that he must have observed her closely to detect those shades of difference which no one else had noted.

"A little, senor. I went to bed late and rose early. Such times as these tax the endurance. But after a siesta I shall be refreshed."

"You look strong and very healthy."

"Ay, but I am! I am not delicate at all. I can ride all day, and swim—which few of our women do. I even like to walk; and I can dance every night for a week. Only, this is an unusual time."

Her supple elastic figure and healthy whiteness of skin betokened endurance and vitality, and he looked at her with pleasure. "Yes, you are strong," he said. "You look as if you would *last*,—as if you never would grow brown nor stout."

"What difference, if the next generation be beautiful?" she said, lightly. "Look at Don Juan de la Borrasca. See him gaze upon Panchita Lopez, who is just sixteen. What does he care that the women of his day are coffee-colored and stringy or fat? You will care as little when you too are brown and dried up, afraid to eat dulces, and each month seeking a new parting for your hair."

"You are a hopeful seer! But you—are you resigned to the time when even the withered old beau will not look at you,—you who are the loveliest woman in the Californias?"

It was the first compliment he had paid her, and she looked up with a swift blush, then lowered her eyes again. "With truth, I never imagine myself except as I am now; but I should have always my books, and no husband to teach me that there were other women more fair."

"And books will suffice, then?"

"Sure." She said it a little wistfully. Then she added, abruptly, "I shall go to confession this week."

"Ah!"

"Yes; for although I hate you still—that is, I do not like you—I have forgiven you. I believe you to be kind and generous, although the enemy of my brother; that if you did oppose him and cast him into prison, you did so with a loyal motive; you cannot help making mistakes, for you are but human. And I do not forget that if it were not for you he would not be a bridegroom to-day. Also, you are not responsible for being an Estenega; so, although I do not forgive the blood in you,—how could I, and be worthy to bear the name of Iturbi y Moncada?—I forgive you, yourself, for being what you cannot help, and for what you have unwittingly and mistakenly done. Do you understand?"

"I understand. Your subtleties are magnificent."

"You must not laugh at me. Tell me, how do you like my friend Valencia?"

"Well enough. I want to hear more about your confession. You fall back into the bosom of your Church with joy, I suppose?"

"Ay!"

"And you would never disobey one of her mandates?"

"Holy God! no."

"Why?"

"Why? Because I am a Catholic."

"That is not what I asked you. Why are you a Catholic? if I must make myself more plain. Why are you afraid to disobey? Why do you cling to the Church with your back braced against your intelligence? It is hope of future reward, I suppose,—or fear?"

"Sure. I want to go to the heaven of the good Catholic."

"Do not waste this life, particularly the youth of it, preparing for a legendary hereafter. Granting, for the sake of argument, that this existence is supplemented by another: you have no knowledge of what elements you will be composed when you lay aside your mortal part to enter there. Your power of enjoyment may be very thin indeed, like the music of a band without brass; the sort of happiness one can imagine a human being to experience out of whose anatomy the nervous system has by some surgical triumph been removed, and in whom love of the arts alone exists, abnormally cultivated. But one thing we of earth do know; you do not, but I will tell you; we have a slight capacity for happiness and a large capacity for enjoyment. There is not much in life, God knows, but there is something. One can get a reasonable amount out of it with due exercise of philosophy. Of that we are sure. Of what comes after we are absolutely unsure."

She had endeavored to interrupt him once or twice, and did so now, her eyes flashing. "Are you an atheist?" she demanded, abruptly. "Are you not a Catholic?"

"I am neither an atheist nor a Catholic. The question of religion has no interest for me whatever. I wish it had none for you."

She looked at him sternly. For a moment I thought the Doomswoman would annihilate the renegade. But her face softened suddenly. "I will pray for you," she said, and turned to the man at her right.

Estenega's face turned the chalky hue I always dreaded, and he bent his lips to her ear.

"Pray for me many times a day; and at other times recall what I said about the relative value of possible and improbable heavens. You are a woman who thinks."

"Don Diego," exclaimed Valencia, unable to control her

impatience longer, and turning sharply from the caballero who was talking to her in a fiery undertone, "thou hast not spoken to me for ten minutes."

"For ten hours, senorita. Thou hast treated me with the scorn and indifference of one weary of homage."

She blushed with gratification. "It is thou who hast forgotten me."

"Would that I could!"

"Dost thou wish to?"

"When I am away from thee, or thou talkest to other men,— sure."

"It is thy fault if I talk to other men."

"You make me feel the Good Samaritan."

"But I care not to talk to them."

"Thy heart is a comb of honey, senorita. On my knees I accept the little morsel the queen bee—thy swift messenger—brings me. Truly, never was sweet so sweetly sweet."

"It is thou who hast the honey on thy tongue, although I fear there may be a stone in thy heart."

"Ah! Why? No stone could sit so lightly in my breast as my heart when those red lips smile to me."

Chonita listened to this conversation with mingled amazement and anger. She did not doubt Estenega's sincerity to herself; neither did Valencia appear to doubt him. But his present levity was manifest to her. Why should he care to talk so to another woman? How strange were men! She gave up the problem.

After the long banquet concluded, the cavalcade formed once more, and we returned to the town. Prudencia rode her white horse alone this time, her husband beside her. Leading the cavalcade was the Presidio band. Its members wore red jackets trimmed with yellow cord, Turkish trousers of white wool, and red Polish caps. With their music mingled the regular detonations of the Presidio cannon. After we had wound the length of the valley we made a progress through the town for the benefit of the populace, who ran to the corridors to watch us, and shouted with delight. But the sun was hot, and we were all glad to be between the thick adobe walls once more.

We took a long siesta that day, but hours before dark the populace was crowded in the court-yard under the booth which had been erected during the afternoon. After the early supper the guests of Casa Grande, and our neighbors of the town, filled the sala, the large bare rooms adjoining, and the corridors. The old people of both degrees seated themselves in rows against the wall, the fiddles scraped, the guitars twanged, the flutes cooed, and the dancing began.

In the court-yard a small space was cleared, and changing couples danced El Jarabe and La Jota,—two stately jigs,—whilst the spectators applauded with wild and impartial enthusiasm, and Don Guillermo from the corridor threw silver coins at the dancers' feet. Now and again a pretty girl would dance alone, her gay skirt lifted with the tips of her fingers, her eyes fixed upon the ground. A man would approach from behind and place his hat on her head. Perhaps she would toss it saucily aside, perhaps let it rest on her coquettish braids,—a token that its owner was her accepted gallant for the evening.

Above, the slender men and women of the aristocracy, the former in black and white, the latter in gowns of vivid richness, danced the contradanza, the most graceful dance I have ever seen; and since those Californian days I have lived in almost every capital of Europe. The music is so monotonous and sweet, the figures so melting and harmonious, that to both spectator and dancer comes a dreaming languid contentment, as were the senses swimming on the brink of sleep. Chonita and Valencia were famous rivals in its rendering, always the sala-stars to those not dancing. Valencia was the perfection of grace, but it was the grace now of the snake, again of the cat. She suggested fangs and claws, a repressed propensity to sudden leaps. Chonita's grace was that of rhythmical music imprisoned in a woman's form of proportions so perfect that she seemed to dissolve from one figure into another, swaying, bending, gliding. The soul of grace emanated from her, too evanescent to be seen, but felt as one feels perfume or the something that is not color in the heart of a rose. Her star-like eyes were open, but the brain behind them was half asleep: she danced by instinct.

I was watching the dancing of these two,—the poetry of promise and the poetry of death,—when suddenly Don Guillermo entered the room, stamped his foot, pulled out his rosary, and instantly we all went down on our knees. It was eight of the clock, and this ceremony was never omitted in Casa Grande, be the occasion festive or domestic. When we had told our beads, Don Guillermo rose, put his rosary in his pocket, trotted out, and the dancing was resumed.

As the contradanza and its ensuing waltz finished, Estenega went up to Chonita. "You are too tired to dance any more tonight," he said. "Let us sit here and talk. Besides, I do not

The Doomswoman   117

like to see you whirling about the room in men's arms."

"It is nothing to you if I dance with other men," she said, rebelliously, although she took the seat he indicated. "And to dance is not wrong."

"Nothing is wrong. In some countries the biggest liar is king. We know as little of ethics—except, to be sure, the ethics of civilization—as one sex knows of another. So we fall back on instinct. I have not a prejudice, but I feel it disgusting to see a woman who is somewhat more to me than other women, embraced by another man. It would infuriate me if done in private; why should it not at least disgust me in public? I care as little for the approving seal of the conventions as I care whether other women—including my own sisters—waltz or not."

And, alas! from that night Chonita never waltzed again. "It is not that I care for his opinion," she assured me later; "only he made me feel that I never wanted a man to touch me again."

Valencia used every art of flashing eyes and pouting lips and gay sally—there was nothing subtle in her methods—to win Estenega to her side; but the sofa on which he sat with Chonita might have been the remotest star in the firmament. Then, prompted by pique and determination to find ointment for her wounded vanity, she suddenly opened her batteries upon Reinaldo. That beautiful young bridegroom was bored to the verge of dissolution by his solemn and sleepy Prudencia, who kept her wide eyes upon him with an expression of rapt adoration, exactly as she regarded the Stations in the Mission when performing the Via Crucis. Valencia, to his mind, was the handsomest woman in the room, and he felt the flattery of her assault. Besides, he was safely married. So he drifted to her side, danced with her, flirted with her, devoted himself to her caprices, until every one was noting, and I thought that Prudencia would bawl outright. Just in the moment, however, when our nerves were humming, Don Guillermo thumped on the door with his stick and ordered us all to go to bed.

XIX

The next morning we started at an early hour for the Rancho de las Rocas, three leagues from Santa Barbara. The populace remained in the booth, but we were joined by all our friends of the town, and once more were a large party. We were bound for a merienda and a carnesada, where bullocks would be roasted whole on spits over a bed of coals in a deep excavation. It took a Californian only a few hours to sleep off fatigue, and we were as fresh and gay as if we had gone to bed at eight the night before.

Valencia managed to ride beside Estenega, and I wondered if she would win him. Woman's persistence, allied to man's vanity, so often accomplishes the result intended by the woman. It seemed to me the simplest climax for the unfolding drama, although I should have been sorry for Diego.

It was Reinaldo's turn to look black, but he devoted himself ostentatiously to Prudencia, who beamed like a child with a stick of candy. Chonita rode between Don Juan de la Borrasca and Adan. Her face was calm, but it occurred to me that she was growing careless of her sovereignty, for her manner was abstracted and indifferent; she seemed to have discarded those little coquetries which had sat so gracefully upon her. Still, as long as she concealed the light of her mind under a bushel, her beauty and Lorleian fascination would draw men to her feet and keep them there. Every man but Estenega and Alvarado was as gay of color as the wild flowers had been, and the girls, as they cantered, looked like full-blown roses. Chonita wore a dark-blue gown and reboso of thin silk, which became her fairness marvelously well.

"Dona Chonita, light of my eyes," said Don Juan, "thou art not wont to be so quiet when I am by thee."

"Thou usually hast enough to say for two."

"Ay, thou canst appreciate the art of speech. Hast thou ever known any one who could converse with lighter ease than I and thy brother?"

"I never have heard any one use more words."

"Ay! they roll from my tongue—and from Reinaldo's—like wheels downhill."

She turned to Adan: "They will be happy, you think,—Reinaldo and Prudencia?"

"Ay!"

"What a beautiful wedding, no?"

"Ay!"

"Life is always the same with thee, I suppose,—smoking, riding, swinging in the hammock?"

"Ay!"

"Thou wouldst not exchange thy life for another? Thou dost not wish to travel?"

"No,—sure."

She wheeled suddenly and galloped over to her father and Alvarado, her caballeros staring helplessly after her.

When we arrived at the rancho the bullocks were already swinging in the pits, the smell of roast meat was in the air. We dismounted, throwing our bridles to the vaqueros in waiting; and while Indian servants spread the table, the girls joined hands and danced about the pit, throwing flowers upon the bullocks, singing and laughing. The men watched them, or amused themselves in various ways,—some with cockfights and impromptu races; others began at once to gamble on a large flat stone; a group stood about a greased pole and jeered at two rival vaqueros endeavoring to mount it for the sake of the gold piece on the top. One buried a rooster in the ground, leaving its head alone exposed; others, mounting their horses, dashed by at full speed, snatching at the head as they passed. Reinaldo distinguished himself by twisting it off with facile wrist while urging his horse to the swiftness of the east wind.

"I am going to dare more than Californian has ever dared before," said Estenega to me, as we gathered at length about the table-cloth. "I am going to get Dona Chonita off by herself in that little canon and have a talk with her. Now, do you stand guard."

"I shall not!" I exclaimed. "It is understood that when Dona Trinidad stays at home Chonita is in my charge. I will not permit such a thing."

"Thou wilt, my Eustaquia. Dona Chonita is no pudding-brained girl. She needs no duena."

"I know that; but it is not that I am thinking of. Suppose

some one sees you; thou knowest the inflexibility of our conventions."

"You forget that we are *comadre* and *compadre*. Our privileges are many." He abruptly dismissed the intimate "thou," with his usual American perversity.

"True; I had forgotten. But whither is all this tending, Diego? She neither will nor can marry you."

"She both can and will. Will you help me, or not? Because if not I shall proceed without you. Only you can make it easier."

I always gave way to him; everybody did.

He was as good as his word. How he managed, Chonita never knew, but not a half-hour after dinner she found herself alone in the canon with him, seated among the huge stones cataclysms had hurled there.

"Why have you brought me here?" she asked.

"To talk with you."

"But this would be severely censured."

"Do you care?"

"No."

She looked at him with a curious feeling she had had before; there was something inside of his head that she wanted to get at,—something that baffled and teased and allured her. She wanted to understand him, and she was oppressed by the weight of her ignorance; she had no key to unlock a man like that. With one of her swift impulses she told him of what she was thinking.

He smiled, his eyes lighting. "I am more than willing you should know all that you would be curious about," he said. "Ask me a hundred questions; I will answer them."

She meditated a moment. She never had taken sufficient interest in a man before to desire to fathom him, and the arts of the Californian belle were not those of the tactfully and impartially interested woman of to-day. She did not know how to begin.

"What have you read?" she asked, at length.

He gave her some account of his library,—a large one,—and mentioned many books of many nations, of which she had never heard.

"You have read all those books?"

"There are many long winter nights and days in the redwood forests of the northern coast."

"That does not tell me much,—what you have read. I feel that it is but one of the many items which went to the making up of you. You have traveled everywhere, no? Was it like living over again the books of travel?"

"Not in the least. Each man travels for himself."

"Madame de Stael said that traveling was sad. Is it so?"

"To the lover of history it is like food without salt: imagination has painted an historical city with the panorama of a great time; it has been to us a stage for great events. We find it a stage with familiar paraphernalia, and actors as commonplace as ourselves."

"It is more satisfactory to stay at home and read about it?"

"Infinitely, though less expanding."

"Then is anything worth while except reading?

"Several things; the pursuit of glory, for one thing, and the active occupied life necessary for its achievement."

She leaned forward a little; she felt that she had stumbled nearer to him. "Are you ambitious?" she asked.

"For what it compels life to yield; abstractly, not. Ambition is the looting of hell in chase of biting flames swirling above a desert of ashes. As for posthumous fame, it must be about as satisfactory as a draught of ice-water poured down the throat of a man who has died on Sahara. And yet, even if in the end it all means nothing, if 'from hour to hour we ripe and ripe and then from hour to hour we rot and rot,' still for a quarter-century or so the nettle of ambition flagellating our brain may serve to make life less uninteresting and more satisfactory. The abstraction and absorption of the fight, the stinging fear of rivals, the murmur of acknowledgment, the shout of compelled applause,—they fill the blanks."

"Tell me," she said, imperiously, "what do you want?"

"Shall I tell you? I never have spoken of it to a living soul but Alvarado. Shall I tell it to a woman,—and an Iturbi y Moncada? Could the folly of man further go?"

"If I am a woman I am an Iturbi y Moncada, and if I am an Iturbi y Moncada I have the honor of its generations in my veins."

"Very good. I believe you would not betray me, even in the interest of your house. Would you?"

"No."

"And I love to talk to you, to tell you what I would tell no other. Listen, then. An envoy goes to Mexico next week with letters from Alvarado, desiring that I be the next governor of the Californias, and containing the assurance that the Departmental Junta will endorse me. I shall follow next month to see Santa Ana personally; I know him well, and he was a friend of my father's. I wish to be invested with peculiar powers; that is to say, I wish California to be practically overlooked while I am governor and I wish it understood that I shall be governor as long as I please. Alvarado will hold no office under the Americans, and is as ready to retire now as a few years later. Of course my predilection for the Americans must be carefully concealed both from the Mexican government and the mass of the people here: Santa Ana and Alvarado know what is bound to come; the Mexicans, generally, retain enough interest in the Californias to wish to keep them. I shall be the last governor of the Department, and I shall employ that period to amalgamate the native population so closely that they will make a strong contingent in the new order of things and be completely under my domination. I shall establish a college with American professors, so that our youth will be taught to think, and to think in English. Alvarado has done something for education, but not enough; he has not enforced it, and the methods are very primitive. I intend to be virtually dictator. With as little delay as possible I shall establish a newspaper,—a powerful weapon in the hands of a ruler, as well as a factor of development. Then I shall organize a superior court for the punishment of capital crimes. Not that

I do not recognize the right of a man to kill if his reasons satisfy himself, but there can be no subservience to authority in a country where murder is practically licensed. American immigration will be more than encouraged, and it shall be distinctly understood by the Americans that I encourage it. Everything, of course, will be done to promote good-will between the Californians and the new-comers. Then, when the United States make up their mind to take possession of us, I shall waste no blood, but hand over a country worthy of capture. In the meantime it will have been carefully drilled into the Californian mind that American occupation will be for their ultimate good, and that I shall go to Washington to protect their interests. There will then be no foolish insurrections. Do you care to hear more?"

Her face was flushed, her chest was rising rapidly.

"I hardly know what to think,—how I feel. You interest me so much as you talk that I wish you to succeed: I picture your success. And yet it maddens me to hear you talk of the Americans in that way,—also to know that your house will be greater than ours,—that we will be forgotten. But—yes, tell me all. What will you do then?"

"I shall have California, in the first place, scratched for the gold that I believe lies somewhere within her. When that great resource *is* located and developed I shall publish in every American newspaper the extraordinary agricultural advantages of the country. In a word, my object is to make California a great State and its name synonymous with my own. As I told you before, for fame as fame I care nothing; I do not care if I am forgotten on my death-bed; but with my blood biting my veins I must have action while living. Shall I say that I have a worthier motive in wishing to aid in the development of civilization? But why worthier? Merely a higher form of selfishness. The best and the worst of motives are prompted by the same instinct."

"I would advise you," she said, slowly, "never to marry. Your wife would be very unhappy."

"But no one has greater scorn than you for the man who spends his life with his lips at the chalice of the poppy."

"True, I had forgotten them." She rose abruptly. "Let us go back," she said. "It is better not to stay too long."

As they walked down the canon she looked at him furtively. The men of her race were almost all tall and finely-proportioned, but they did not suggest strength as this man did. And his face,—it was so grimly determined at times that she shrank from it, then drew near, fascinated. It had no beauty at all—according to Californian standards; she could not know that it represented all that intellect, refinement and civilization, generally, would do for the human race for a century to come,—but it had a subtle power, an absolute audacity, an almost contemptuous fearlessness in its bold, fine outline, a dominating intelligence in the keen deeply-set eyes, and a hint of weakness, where and what she could not determine, that mystified and magnetized her.

"I know you a little better," she said, "just a little,—enough to make my curiosity ache and jump. At the same time, I know now what I did not before,—that I might climb and mine and study and watch, and you would always be beyond me. There is something subtle and evasive about you— something I seem to be close to always, yet never can see or grasp."

"It is merely the barrier of sex. A man can know a woman fairly well, because her life, consequently the interests which mould her mind and conceive her thoughts, are more or less simple. A man's life is so complex, his nature so inevitably the sum and work of it of it lies so far outside of woman's sphere, his mind spiked with a thousand magnets, each pointing to a different possibility,—that she would need divine wisdom to comprehend him in his entirety, even if he made her a diagram of every cell in his brain,—which he never would, out of consideration for both her and his own vanity. But within certain restrictions there can be a magnificent sense of comradeship."

"But a woman, I think, would never be happy with that something in the man always beyond her grasp,—that something which she could be nothing to. She would be more jealous of that independence of her in man than of another woman."

"That was pure insight," he said. "You could not know that."

"No," she said, "I had not thought of it before."

I had made a martyr of myself on a three-cornered stone at the entrance of the canon, waiting to duena them out. "Never will I do this again!" I exclaimed, with that virtue born of discomfort, as they came in sight.

"My dearest Eustaquia," said Diego, kissing my hand gallantly, "thou hast given me pleasure so often, most charming and clever of women, thou hast but added one new art to thy overflowing store."

We mounted almost immediately upon returning, and I was alone with Chonita for a moment. "Do you realize that you are playing with fire?" I said, warningly. "Estenega is a dangerous man; the most successful man with women I have ever known."

"I do not deny his power," she said. "But I am safe, for the many reasons thou knowest of. And, being safe, why should I deny myself the pleasure of talking to him? I shall never meet his like again. Let me live for a little while."

"Ay, but do not live too hard! It hurts down into the core and marrow."

XX

While we were eating supper, a dozen Indian girls were gathered about a table in one of the large rooms behind the house, busily engaged in blowing out the contents of several hundred eggs and filling the hollowed shells with cologne, flour, tinsel, bright scraps of paper. Each egg-was then sealed with white wax, and ready for the cascaron frolic of the evening.

We had been dancing, singing, and talking for an hour after rosario, when the eggs were brought in. In an instant every girl's hair was unbound, a wild dive was made for the great trays, and eggs flew in every direction. Dancing was forgotten. The girls and men chased each other about the room, the air was filled with perfume and glittering particles, the latter looking very pretty on black floating hair. Etiquette demanded that only one egg should be thrown by the same hand at a time, but quick turns of supple wrists followed each other very rapidly. To really accomplish a feat the egg must crash on the back of the head, and each occupied in attack was easy prey.

Chonita was like a child. Two priests were of our party, and she made a target of their shaven crowns, shrieking with delight. They vowed revenge, and chased her all over the house; but not an egg had broken on that golden mane. She was surrounded at one time by caballeros, but she whirled and doubled so swiftly that every cascaron flew afield.

The pelting grew faster and more furious; every room was invaded; we chased each other up and down the corridors. The people in the court had their cascarones also, and the noise must have been heard at the Mission. Don Guillermo hobbled about delightedly, covered with tinsel and flour. Estenega had tried a dozen times to hit Chonita, but as if by instinct she faced him each time before the egg could leave his hand. Finally he pursued her down the corridor to her library, where I, fortunately, happened to be resting, and both threw themselves into chairs, breathless.

"Let us stay here," he said. "We have had enough of this."

"Very well," she said. She bent her head to lift a book which had fallen from a shelf, and felt the soft blow of the cascaron.

"At last!" said Estenega, contentedly. "I was determined to conquer, if I waited until morning."

Chonita looked vexed for a moment,—she did not like to be vanquished,—then shrugged her shoulders and leaned back in her chair. The little room was plainly furnished. Shelves covered three sides, and the window-seat and the table were littered with books. There were no curtains, no ornaments; but Chonita's hair, billowing to the floor, her slender voluptuous form, her white skin and green irradiating eyes, the candlelight half revealing, half concealing, made a picture requiring no background. I caught the expression of Estenega's face, and determined to remain if he murdered me.

Peals of laughter, joyous shrieks, screams of mock terror, floated in to us. I broke a silence which was growing awkward:

"How happy they are! Creatures of air and sunshine! Life in this Arcadia is an idyl."

"They are not happy," said Estenega, contemptuously; "they are gay. They are light of heart through absence of material cares and endless sources of enjoyment, which in turn have bred a careless order of mind. But did each pause long enough to look into his own heart, would he not find a stone somewhere in its depths?—perhaps a skull graven on the stone,—who knows?"

"Oh, Diego!" I exclaimed, impatiently, "this is a party, not a funeral."

"Then is no one happy?" asked Chonita, wistfully.

"How can he be, when in each moment of attainment he is pricked by the knowledge that it must soon be over? The youth is not happy, because the shadow of the future is on him. The man is not happy, because the knowledge of life's incompleteness is with him."

"Then of what use to live at all?"

"No use. It is no use to die, neither, so we live. I will grant that there may be ten completely happy moments in life,— the ten conscious moments preceding certain death—and oblivion."

"I will not discuss the beautiful hope of our religion with you, because you do not believe, and I should only get angry. But what are we to do with this life? You say nothing is wrong nor right. What would you have the stumbling and unanchored do with what has been thrust upon him?"

"Man, in his gropings down through the centuries, has

concocted, shivered, and patched certain social conditions well enough calculated to develop the best and the worst that is in us, making it easier for us to be bad than good, that good might be the standard. We feel a deeper satisfaction if we have conquered an evil impulse and done what is accepted as right, because we have groaned and stumbled in the doing,—that is all. Temptation is sweet only because the impulse comes from the depths of our being, not because it is difficult to be tempted. If we overcome, the satisfaction is deep and enduring,—which only goes to show that man is but a petty egotist, always drawing pictures of himself on a pedestal. The man who emancipates himself from traditions and yields to his impulses is debarred from happiness by the blunders of the blindfolded generations preceding him, which arranged that to yield was easy and to resist difficult. Had they reversed the conditions and conclusions, the majority of the human race would have fought each other to death, but the selected remnant would have had a better time of it.

"Let us suppose a case as conditions now exist. Assume, for the sake of argument, that you loved me and that you plucked from your nature your religion, your fidelity to your house, your love for your brother, and gave yourself to me. You would stand appalled at the sacrifice until you realized that you had come to me only because it would have been more difficult to stay away. You conquer the passionate cry of love,—the strongest the human compound has ever voiced,—and you are miserably happy for the rest of your life no attitude being so pleasing to the soul as the attitude of martyrdom. Many a man and woman looks with some impatience for the last good-bye to be said, so sweet is the prospect of sadness, of suffering, of resignation."

I was aghast at his audacity, but I saw that Chonita was fascinated. Her egotism was caressed, and her womanhood thrilled. "Are we all such shams as that?" was what she said. "You make me despise myself."

"Not yourself, but a great structure—of which you are but a grain—with a faulty foundation. Don't despise yourself. Curse the builders who shoveled those stones together."

He left her then, and she told me to go to bed; she wanted to sit a while and think.

"He makes you think too much," I said. "Better forget what he says as soon as you can. He is a very disturbing influence."

But she made me no reply, and sat there staring at the floor. She began to feel a sense of helplessness, like a creature caught in a net. It was more the man's personality than his words which made her feel as if he were pouring himself throughout her, taking possession of brain and every sense, as though he were a sort of intellectual drug.

"I believe I was made from his rib," she thought, angrily, "else why can he have this extraordinary power over me? I do not love him. I have read somewhat of love, and seen more. This is different, quite. I only feel that there is something in him that I want. Sometimes I feel that I must dig my nails into him and tear him apart until I find what I want,—something that belongs to me. Sometimes it is as if he promised it, at others as if he were unconscious of its existence; always it is evanescent. Is he going to make my mind his own?—and yet he always seems to leave mine free. He has never snubbed me. He makes me think: there is the danger."

An hour later there was a tap on her door. Casa Grande was asleep. She sat upright, her heart beating rapidly. Estenega was audacious enough for anything. But it was her brother who entered.

"Reinaldo!" she exclaimed, horrified to feel an unmistakable stab of disappointment.

"Yes, it is I. Art thou alone?"

"Sure."

"I have something to say to thee."

He drew a chair close to her and sat down "Thou knowest, my sister," he began, haltingly, "how I hate the house of Estenega. My hatred is as loyal as thine: every drop of blood in my veins is true to the honor of the house of Iturbi y Moncada. But, my sister, is it not so that one can sacrifice himself, his mere personal feelings, upon the altar of his country? Is it not so, my sister?"

"What is it thou wishest me to understand, Reinaldo?"

"Do not look so stern, my Chonita. Thou hast not yet heard me; and, although thou mayest be angry then, thou wilt reason later. Thou art devoted to thy house, no?"

"Thou hast come here in the night to ask me such a question as that?"

"And thou lovest thy brother?"

"Reinaldo, thou hast drunken more mescal than Angelica. Go back to thy bride." But, although she spoke lightly, she was uneasy.

"My sister, I never drank a drop of mescal in my life! Listen.

It is our father's wish, thy wish, my wish, that I become a great and distinguished man, an ornament to the house of Iturbi y Moncada, a star on the brow of California. How can I accomplish this great and desirable end? By the medium of politics only; our wars are so insignificant. I have been debarred from the Departmental Junta by the enemy of our house, else would it have rung with my eloquence, and Mexico have known me to-day. Yet I care little for the Junta. I wish to go as diputado to Mexico; it is a grander arena. Moreover, in that great capital I shall become a man of the world,—which is necessary to control men. That is *his* power,—curse him! And he—he will not let me go there. Even Alvarado listens to him. The Departmental Junta is under his thumb. I will never be anything but a caballero of Santa Barbara—I, an Iturbi y Moncada, the last scion of a line illustrious in war, in diplomacy, in politics—until he is either dead—do not jump, my sister; it is not my intention to murder him and ruin my career—or becomes my friend."

"Canst thou not put thy meaning in fewer words?"

"My sister, he loves thee, and thou lovest thy brother and thy house."

Chonita rose to her full height, and although he rose too, and was taller, she seemed to look down upon him.

"Thou wouldst have me marry him? Is that thy meaning?"

"Ay." His voice trembled. Under his swagger he was always a little afraid of the Doomswoman.

"Thou askest perjury and disloyalty and dishonor of an Iturbi y Moncada?"

"An Iturbi y Moncada asks it of an Iturbi y Moncada. If the

man is ready to bend his neck in sacrifice to the glory of his house, is it for the woman to think?"

Chonita stood grasping the back of her chair convulsively; it was the only sign of emotion she betrayed. She knew that what he said was true: that Estenega, for public and personal reasons, never would let him go to Mexico; he would permit no enemy at court. But this knowledge drifted through her mind and out of it at the moment; she was struggling to hold down a hot wave of contempt rushing upward within her. She clung to her traditions as frantically as she clung to her religion.

"Go," she said, after a moment.

"Thou wilt think of what I have said?"

"I shall pray to forget it."

"Chonita!" his voice rang out so loud that she placed her hand on his mouth. He dashed it away. "Thou wilt!" he cried, like a spoilt child. "Thou wilt! I shall go to the city of Mexico, and only thou canst send me there. All my father's gold and leagues will not buy me a seat in the Mexican Congress, unless this accursed Estenega lifts his hand and says, 'Thou shalt.' Holy God! how I hate him! Would that I had the chance to murder him! I would cut his heart out to-morrow. And my father likes him, and has outlived rancor. And thou—thou art not indifferent."

"Go!"

He threw his arms about her, kissing and caressing her. "My sister! My sister! Thou wilt! Say that thou wilt!" But she flung him off as if he were a snake.

"Wilt thou go?" she asked.

"Ay! I go. But he shall suffer. I swear it! I swear it!" And he rushed from the room.

Chonita sat there, staring more fixedly at the floor than when Estenega had left her.

XXI

Reinaldo did not go to his Prudencia. He went down to the booths in the town and joined the late revelers. Don Guillermo, rising before dawn, and walking up and down the corridor to conquer the pangs of Dona Trinidad's dulces, noticed that the door of his son's room was ajar. He paused before it and heard slow, regular, patient sobs. He opened the door and went in. Prudencia, alone, curled up in a far corner of her bed, the clothes over her head, was bemoaning many things incidental to matrimony. As she heard the sound of heavy steps she gave a little shriek.

"It is I, Prudencia," said her uncle. "Where is Reinaldo?"

"I—do—not—know."

"Did he not come from the ball-room with thee?"

"N-o-o-o-o."

"Dost thou know where he has gone?"

"N-o-o-o, senor."

"Art thou afraid?"

"Ay! God—of—my—life!"

"Never mind," said the old gentleman. "Go to sleep. Thy uncle will protect thee, and this will not happen again."

He seated himself by the bedside. Prudencia's sobs ceased gradually, and she fell asleep. An hour later the door opened softly, and Reinaldo entered. In spite of the mescal in him, his knees shook as he saw the indulgent but stern arbiter of the Iturbi y Moncada destinies sitting in judgment at the bedside of his wife.

"Where have you been, sir?"

"To take a walk,—to see to—"

"No lying! It makes no difference where you have been. What I want to know is this: Is it your duty to gallivant about town? or is your place at this hour beside your wife?"

"Here, senor."

The old man rose, and, seizing the bride-groom by the shoulders, shook him until his teeth clattered together. "Then see that you stay here with her hereafter, or you shall no longer be a married man." And he stamped out and slammed the door behind him.

XXII

We spent the next day at the race-field. Many of the caballeros had brought their finest horses, and Reinaldo's were famous. The vaqueros threw off their black glazed sombreros and black velvet jackets, wearing only the short black trousers laced with silver, a shirt of dazzling whiteness, a silk handkerchief twisted about the head, and huge spurs on their bare brown heels. Some of us stood on a platform, others remained on their horses; all were wild with excitement and screamed themselves hoarse. The great dark eyes of the girls flashed, their red mouths trembled with the flood of eager exclamations; the lace mantilla or flowered reboso fluttered against hot cheeks, to be torn off, perhaps, and waved in the enthusiasm of the moment. They forgot the men, and the men forgot them. Even Chonita was oblivious to all else for the hour. She was a famous horsewoman, and keenly alive to the enchantment of the race-field. The men bet their ranchos, whole caponeras of their finest horses, herds of cattle, their saddles and their jewels. Estenega won largely, and, as it happened, from Reinaldo particularly. Don Guillermo was rather pleased than otherwise, holding his son to be in need of further punishment; but Reinaldo was obliged to call upon all the courtesy of the Spaniard and all the falseness of his nature to help him remember that his enemy was his guest.

We went home to siesta and long gay supper, where the races were the only topic of conversation; then to dance and sing and flirt until midnight, the people in the booths as tireless as ourselves. Valencia's attentions to Estenega were as conspicuous as usual, but he managed to devote most of his time to Chonita.

* * * * *

That night Chonita had a dream. She dreamed that she awoke without a soul. The sense of vacancy was awful, yet there was a singular undercurrent consciousness that no soul ever had been within her,—that it existed, but was yet to be found.

She arose, trembling, and opened her door. Santa Barbara was as quiet as all the world is in the chill last hours of night. She half expected to see something hover before her, a will-o'-the-wisp, alluring her over the rocky valleys and towering mountains until death gave her weary feet rest. She remembered vaguely that she had read legends of that purport.

But there was nothing,—not even the glow of a late cigarito or the flash of a falling star. Still she seemed to know where the soul awaited her. She closed her door softly and walked swiftly down the corridor, her bare feet making no sound on the boards. At a door on the opposite side she paused, shaking violently, but unable to pass it. She opened the door and went in. The room, like all the others in that time of festivity, had more occupants than was its wont; a bed was in each corner. The shutters and windows were open, the moonlight streamed in, and she saw that all were asleep. She crossed the room and looked down upon Diego Estenega. His night garment, low about the throat, made his head, with its sharply-cut profile, look like the heads on old Roman medallions. The pallor of night, the extreme refinement of his face, the deep repose, gave him an unmortal appearance. Chonita bent over him fearfully. Was he dead? His breathing was regular, but very quiet. She stood gazing down upon him, the instinct of seeking vanished. What did it mean? Was this her soul! A man? How could it be? Even in poetry she had never read of a man being a woman's soul,—a man with all his frailties and sins, for the most part unrepented. She felt, rather than knew, that Estenega had trampled many laws, and that he cared too little for any law but his own will to repent. And yet, there he lay, looking, in the gray light and the impersonality of sleep, as sinless as if he had been created within the hour. He looked not like a man but a spirit,—a soul; and the soul was hers.

Again she asked herself, what did it mean? Was the soul but brain? She and he were so alike in rudiments, yet he so immeasurably beyond her in experience and knowledge and the stronger fiber of a man's mind—

He awoke suddenly and saw her. For a moment he stared incredulously, then raised himself on his hand.

"Chonita!" he whispered.

But Chonita, with the long glide of the Californian woman, faded from the room.

When she awoke the next morning she was assailed by a distressing fear. Had she been to Estenega's room the night before? The memory was too vivid, the details too practical, for a sleep-vagary. At breakfast she hardly dared to raise her eyes. She felt that he was watching her; but he often watched her. After breakfast they were alone at one end of the corridor for a moment, and she compelled herself to raise her eyes and look at him steadily. He was regarding her searchingly.

She was not a woman to endure uncertainty.

"Tell me," she cried, trembling from head to foot, the blood rushing over her face, "did I go to your room last night?"

"Dona Chonita!" he exclaimed. "What an extraordinary question! You have been dreaming."

XXIII

We went to a bull-fight that day, danced that night, meriendaed and danced again; a siesta in the afternoon, a few hours' sleep in the night, refreshing us all. Chonita, alone, looked pale, but I knew that her pallor was not due to weariness. And I knew that she was beginning to fear Estenega; the time was almost come when she would fear herself more. Estenega had several talks apart with her. He managed it without any apparent maneuvering; but he always had the devil's methods. Valencia avenged herself by flirting desperately with Reinaldo, and Prudencia's honeymoon was seasoned with gall.

On Saturday night Chonita stole from her guests, donned a black gown and reboso, and, attended by two Indian servants, went up to the Mission to confession. As she left the church a half-hour later, and came down the steps, Estenega rose from a bench beneath the arches of the corridor and joined her.

"How did you know that I came?" she asked; and it was not the stars that lit her face.

"You do little that I do not know. Have you been to confession?"

"Yes."

They walked slowly down the valley.

"And you forgave and were forgiven?"

"Yes. Ay! but my penance is heavy!"

"But when it is done you will be at rest, I suppose."

"Oh, I hope! I hope!"

"Have you begun to realize that your Church cannot satisfy you?"

"No! I will not say that."

"But you know it. Your intelligence has opened a window somewhere and the truth has crept in."

"Do not take my religion from me, senor!" Her eyes and voice appealed to him, and he accepted her first confession of weakness with a throb of exulting tenderness.

"My love!" he said, "I would give you more than I took from you."

"No! never!—Even if we were not enemies, and I had not made that terrible vow, my religion has been all in all to me. Just now I have many things that torment me; and I have asked so little of religion before—my life has been so calm—that now I hardly know how to ask for so much more. I shall learn. Leave me in peace."

"Do you want me to go?" he asked. "If you did,—if I troubled you by staying here,—I believe I would go. Only I know it would do no good: I should come back."

"No! no! I do not want you to go. I should feel—I will admit to you—like a house without its foundation. And yet sometimes, I pray that you will go. Ay! I do not like life. I used to have pride in my intelligence. Where is my pride now? What good has the wisdom in my books done me, when I confess my dependence upon a man, and that man my enemy—and the acquaintance of a few weeks?" She was speaking incoherently, and Estenega chafed at the restraint of the servants so close behind them. "Tell me," she exclaimed, "what is it in you that I want?—that I need? It is something that belongs to me. Give it to me, and go away."

"Chonita, I give it to you gladly, God knows. But you must take me, too. You want in me what is akin to you and what you will find nowhere else. But I cannot tear my soul out of my body. You must take both or neither."

"Ay! I cannot! You know that I cannot!"

"I ignore your reasons."

"But I do not."

"You shall, my beloved. Or if you do not ignore you shall forget them."

"When I am dead—would that I were!" She was excited and trembling. The confession had been an ordeal, and Estenega was never tranquillizing. She wished to cling to him, but was still mistress of herself. He divined her impulse, and drew her arm through his and across his breast. He opened her hand and pressed his lips to the palm. Then he bent his face above hers. She was trembling violently; her face was wild and white. His own was ashen, and the heart beneath her arm beat rapidly.

"I love you devotedly," he said. "You believe that, Chonita?"

"Ah! Mother of God! do not! I cannot listen."

"But you shall listen. Throw off your superstitions and come to me. Keep the part of your religion that is not superstition; I would be the last to take it from you; but I will not permit its petty dogmas to stand between us. As for your traditions, you have not even the excuse of filial duty; your father would not forbid you to become my wife. And I love you very earnestly and passionately. Just how much, I might convey to you if we were alone."

He was obliged to exercise great self-restraint, but there was no mistaking his seriousness. When such scientific triflers do find a woman worth loving, they are too deeply sensible of the fact not to be stirred to their depths; and their depths are apt to be in large disproportion to the lightness of their ordinary mood. "Come to me," he continued. "I need you; and I will be as tender and thoughtful a husband as I will be ardent as a lover. You love me: don't blind yourself any longer. Do you picture, in a life of solitude and cold devotion to phantoms, any happiness equal to what you would find here in my arms?"

"Oh, hush! hush! You could make me do what you wished, I have no will. I feel no longer myself. What is this terrible power?"

"It is the magnetism of love; that is all. I am not exercising any diabolical power over you. Listen: I will not trouble you any more now. I am obliged to go to Los Angeles the day after to-morrow, and on my way back to Monterey—in about two weeks—I shall come here again. Then we will talk together; but I warn you, I will accept only one answer. You are mine, and I shall have you."

They reached Casa Grande a moment later, and she escaped from him and ran to her room. But she dared not remain alone. Hastily changing her black gown for the first her hand touched,—it happened to be vivid red and made her look as white as wax,—she returned to the sala; not to dance even the square contradanza, but to stand surrounded by worshiping caballeros with curling hair tied with gay ribbons, and jewels in their laces. Valencia regarded her with a bitter jealousy that was rising from red heat to white. How dared a woman with hair of gold wear the color of the brunette? It was a theft. It was the last indignity. And once more she chained Reinaldo, in default of Estenega, to her side. And deep in Prudencia's heart wove a scheme of vengeance; the loom and warp had been presented unwittingly by her chivalrous father-in-law.

Estenega remained in the sala a few moments after Chonita's reappearance, then left the house and wandered through the booth in the court, where the people were dancing and singing and eating and gambling as if with the morrow an eternal Lent would come, and thence through the silent town to the pleasure-grounds of Casa Grande, which lay about half a mile from the house. He had been there but a short while when he heard a rustle, a light footfall; and, turning, he saw Chonita, unattended, her bare neck and gold hair gleaming against the dark, her train dragging. She was advancing swiftly toward him. His pulses bounded, and he sprang toward her, his arms outstretched; but she waved him back.

"Have mercy," she said. "I am alone. I brought no one, because I have that to tell you which no one else must hear."

He stepped back and looked at the ground.

"Listen," she said. "I could not wait until to-morrow, because a moment lost might mean—might mean the ruin of your career, and you say your envoy has not gone yet. Just now— I will tell you the other first. Mother of God! that I should betray my brother to my enemy! But it seems to me right, because you placed your confidence in me, and I should feel that I betrayed you if I did not warn you. I do not know—oh, Mary!—I do not know—but this seems to me right. The other night my brother came to me and asked me—ay! do not look at me—to marry you, that you would balk his ambition no further. He wishes to go as diputado to Mexico, and he knows that you will not let him. I thought my brain would crack,—an Iturbi y Moncada!—I made him no answer,—there was no answer to a demand like that,—and he went from me in a fury, vowing vengeance upon you. To-night, a few moments ago, he whispered to me that he knew of your plans, your intentions regarding the Americans: he had overheard a conversation between you and Alvarado. He says that he will send letters to Mexico to-morrow, warning the government against you. Then their suspicions will be roused, and they will inquire—Ay, Mary!"

Estenega brought his teeth together. "God!" he exclaimed.

She saw that he had forgotten her. She turned and went back more swiftly than she had come.

Estenega was a man whose resources never failed him. He returned to the house and asked Reinaldo to smoke a cigarito and drink a bottle of wine in his room. Then, without a promise or a compromising word, he so flattered that shallow youth, so allured his ambition and pampered his vanity and watered his hopes, that fear and hatred wondered at their existence, closed their eyes, and went to sleep. Reinaldo poured forth his aspirations, which under the influence of the truth-provoking vine proved to be an honest yearning for the pleasures of Mexico. As he rose to go he threw his arm about Estenega's neck.

"Ay! my friend! my friend!" he cried, "thou art all-powerful. Thou alone canst give me what I want."

"Why did you never ask me for what you wanted?" asked Estenega. And he thought, "If it were not for Her, you would be on your way to Los Angeles to-night under charge of high treason. I would not have taken this much trouble with you."

XXIV

A rodeo was held the next day,—the last of the festivities;— Don Guillermo taking advantage of the gathering of the rancheros. It was to take place on the Cerros Rancho, which adjoined the Rancho de las Rocas. We went early, most of us dismounting and taking to the platform on one side of the circular rodeo-ground. The vaqueros were already galloping over the hills, shouting and screaming to the cattle, who ran to them like dogs; soon a herd came rushing down into the circle, where they were thrown down and branded, the stray cattle belonging to neighbors separated and corralled. This happened again and again, the interest and excitement growing with each round-up.

Once a bull, seeing his chance, darted from his herd and down the valley. A vaquero started after him; but Reinaldo, anxious to display his skill in horsemanship, and being still mounted, called to the vaquero to stop, dashed after the animal, caught it by its tail, spurred his horse ahead, let go the tail at the right moment, and, amidst shouts of "Coliar!" "Coliar!" the bull was ignominiously rolled in the dust, then meekly preceded Reinaldo back to the rodeo-ground.

After the dinner under the trees most of the party returned to the platform, but Estenega, Adan, Chonita, Valencia, and myself strolled about the rancho. Adan walked at Chonita's side, more faithful than her shadow. Valencia's black eyes flashed their language so plainly to Estenega's that he could not have deserted her without rudeness; and Estenega never was rude.

"Adan," said Chonita, abruptly, "I am tired of thee. Sit down under that tree until I come back. I wish to walk alone with Eustaquia for awhile."

Adan sighed and did as he was bidden, consoling himself with a cigarito. Taking a different path from the one the others followed, we walked some distance, talking of ordinary matters, both avoiding the subject of Diego Estenega by common consent. And yet I was convinced that she carried on a substratum of thought of which he was the subject, even while she talked coherently to me. On our way back the conversation died for want of bone and muscle, and, as it happened, we were both silent as we approached a small adobe hut. As we turned the corner we came upon Estenega and Valencia. He had just bent his head and kissed her.

Valencia fled like a hare. Estenega turned the hue of chalk, and I knew that blue lightning was flashing in his disconcerted brain. I felt the chill of Chonita as she lifted herself to the rigidity of a statue and swept slowly down the path.

"Diego, you are a fool!" I exclaimed, when she was out of hearing.

"You need not tell me that," he said, savagely. "But what in heaven's name—Well, never mind. For God's sake straighten it out with her. Tell her—explain to her—what men are. Tell her that the present woman is omnipotently present—no, don't tell her that. Tell her that history is full of instances of men who have given one woman the devoted love of a lifetime and been unfaithful to her every week in the year. Explain to her that a man to love one woman must love all women. And she has sufficient proof that I love her and no other woman: I want to marry her, not Valencia Menendez. Heaven knows I will be true to her when I have her. I could not be otherwise. But I need not explain to you. Set it right with her. She has brain, and can be made to understand."

I shook my head. "You cannot reason with inexperience; and when it is allied to jealousy—God of my soul! Her ideal, of course, is perfection, and does not take human weakness into account. You have fallen short of it to-day. I fear your cause is lost."

"It is not! Do you think I will give her up for a trifle like that?"

"But why not accept this break? You cannot marry her—"

"Oh, do not refer to that nonsense!" he exclaimed, harshly. "I shall peel off her traditions when the time comes, as I would strip off the outer hulls of a nut. Go! Go, Eustaquia!"

Of course I went. Chonita was not at the rodeo-ground, but, escorted by her father, had gone home. I followed immediately, and when I reached Casa Grande I found her sitting in her library. I never saw a statue look more like marble. Her face was locked: only the eyes betrayed the soul in torment. But she looked as immutable as a fate.

"Chonita," I exclaimed, hardly knowing where to begin, "be reasonable. Men of Estenega's brain and passionate affectionate nature are always weak with women, but it means nothing. He cares nothing for Valencia Menendez. He is madly in love with you. And his weakness, my dear, springs from the same source as his charm. He would not be the man he is without it. His heart would be less kindly, his impulses less generous, his brain less virile, his sympathies less instinctive and true. The strong impregnable man, the man whom no vice tempts, no weakness assails, who is loyal without effort,—such a man lacks breadth and magnetism and the power to read the human heart and sympathize with both its noble impulses and its terrible weaknesses. Such men—I never have known it to fail—are full of petty vanities and egoisms and contemptible weaknesses, the like of which Estenega could not be capable of. No man can be perfect, and it is the man of great strength and great weakness who alone understands and sympathizes with human nature, who is lovable and magnetic, and who has the power to rouse the highest as well as the most passionate love of a woman. Such men cause infinite suffering, but they can give a happiness that makes the suffering worth while. You never will meet another man like Diego Estenega. Do not cast him lightly aside."

"Do I understand," said Chonita, in a perfectly unmoved voice, "that you are counseling me to marry an Estenega and the man who would send me to Hell hereafter? Do you forget my vow?"

I came to myself with a shock. In the enthusiasm of my defense I had forgotten the situation.

"At least forgive him," I said, lamely.

"I have nothing to forgive," she said. "He is nothing to me."

I knew that it was useless to argue with her.

"I have a favor to ask of you," she said. "Most of our guests leave this afternoon: will you let me sleep alone to-night?"

I should have liked to put my arm about her and give her a woman's sympathy, but I did not dare. All I could do was to leave her alone.

XXV

Casa Grande held three jealous women. The situation had its comic aspect, but was tragic enough to the actors.

In the evening the lingering guests of the house and the neighbors of the town assembled as usual for the dance. Only Estenega absented himself. Valencia stood her ground: she would not go while Estenega remained. Chonita moved proudly among her guests, and never had been more gracious. Valencia dared not meet her eyes nor mine, but, seeing that Prudencia was watching her, avenged her own disquiet by enhancing that of the bride. Never did she flirt so imperiously with Reinaldo as she did that fateful night; and Reinaldo, who was man's vanity collected and compounded, devoted himself to the dashing beauty. Her cheeks burned with excitement, her eyes were restless and flashing.

The music stopped. The women were eating the dulces passed by the Indian servants. The men had not yet gone into the dining-room. Valencia dropped her handkerchief; Reinaldo, stooping to recover it, kissed her hand behind its flimsy shelter.

Then Prudencia arose. She trailed her long gown down the room between the two rows of people staring at her grim eyes and pressed lips; her little head, with its high comb, stiffly erect. She walked straight up to Reinaldo and boxed his ears before the assembled company.

"Thou wilt flirt no more with other women," she said, in a loud, clear voice. "Thou art my husband, and thou wilt not forget it again. Come with me."

And, amidst the silence of mountain-tops in a snow-storm, he stumbled to his feet and followed her from the room.

I could not sleep that night. In spite of the amusement I had felt at Prudencia's *coup-d'etat*, I was oppressed by the chill and foreboding which seemed to emanate from Chonita and pervade the house. I knew that terrible calm was like the menacing stillness of the hours before an earthquake. What would she do in the coming convulsion? I shuddered and tormented myself with many imaginings.

I became so nervous that I rose and dressed and went out upon the corridor and walked up and down. It was very late, and the moon was risen, but the corners were dark. Figures seemed to start from them, but my nerves were strong; I never had given way to fear.

My thoughts wandered to Estenega. Who shall judge the complex heart of a man? the deep, intense, lasting devotion he may have for the one woman he recognizes as his soul's own, and yet the strange wayward wanderings of his fancy,—the nomadic assertion of the animal; the passionate love he may feel for this woman of all women, yet the reserve in which he always holds her, never knowing her quite as well as he has known other women; the last test of highest love, passion without sensuality? And yet the regret that she does not gratify every side of his nature, even while he would not have her; regret for the terrible incongruity of human nature, the mingling of the beast and the divine, which cannot find satisfaction in the same woman; whatever the fire in her, she cannot gratify the instincts which rage below passion in man, without losing the purity of mind which he adores in her. She, too, feels a vague regret that some portion of his nature is a sealed book to her, forever beyond her ken. But her regret is nothing to his: he knows, and she does not.

My meditations were interrupted suddenly. I heard a door stealthily opened. I knew before turning that the door was that of Chonita's room, the last at the end of the right wing. It opened, and she came out. It was as if a face alone came out. She was shrouded from head to foot in black, and her face was as white as the moon. Possessed by a nameless but overwhelming fear, I turned the knob of the door nearest me and almost fell into the room. I closed the door behind me, but there was no key. By the strip of white light which entered through the crevice between the half-open shutters I saw that I was in the room of Valencia Menendez; but she slept soundly and had not heard me.

I stood still, listening, for many minutes. At first there was no sound; I evidently had startled her, and she was waiting for the house to be still again. At last I heard some one gliding down the corridor. Then, suddenly, I knew that she was coming to this room, and, possessed by a horrible curiosity and growing terror, I sank on my knees in a corner.

The door opened noiselessly, and Chonita entered. Again I saw only her white face, rigid as death, but the eyes flamed with the terrible passions that her soul had flung up from its depths at last. Then I saw another white object,—her hand. But there was no knife in it. Had there been, I think I should have shaken off the spell which controlled me: I never would see murder done. It was the awe of the unknown that paralyzed my muscles. She bent over Valencia, who moved uneasily and cast her arms above her head. I saw her touch her finger to the sleeping woman's mouth, inserting it between the lips. Then she moved backward and stood by the head of the bed, facing the window. She raised herself to her full height and extended her arms horizontally. The position gave her the form of a cross—a black cross, topped and pointed with malevolent white; one hand was spread above Valencia's face. She was the most awful sight I ever beheld. She uttered no sound; she scarcely breathed. Suddenly, with the curve of a panther, her figure glided above the unconscious woman, her open hand describing a strange motion; then she melted from the room.

Valencia awoke, shrieking.

"Some one has cursed me!" she cried. "Mother of God! Some one has cursed me!"

I fled from the room, to faint upon my own bed.

XXVI

The next morning Casa Grande was thrown into consternation. Valencia Menendez was in a raging fever, and had to be held in her bed.

After breakfast I sent for Estenega and told him of what I had seen. In the first place I had to tell some one, and in the second I thought to end his infatuation and avert further trouble. "You firebrand!" I exclaimed, in conclusion. "You see the mischief you have worked! You will go, now, thank heaven—and go cured."

"I will go,—for a time," he said. "This mood of hers must wear itself out. But, if I loved her before, I worship her now. She is magnificent!—a woman with the passions of hell and the sweetness of an angel. She is the woman I have waited for all my life,—the only woman I have ever known. Some day I will take her in my arms and tell her that I understand her."

"Diego," I said, divided between despair and curiosity, "you have fancied many women: wherein does your feeling for Chonita differ? How can you be sure that this is love? What is your idea of love?"

He sat down and was silent for a moment, then spoke

thoughtfully: "Love is not passion, for one may feel that for many women; not affection, for friendship demands that. Not even sympathy and comradeship; one can find either with men. Nor all, for I have felt all, yet something was lacking. Love is the mysterious turning of one heart to another with the promise of a magnetic harmony, a strange original delight, a deep satisfaction, a surety of permanence, which did either heart roam the world it never would find again. It is the knowledge that did the living body turn to corruption, the spirit within would still hold and sway the steel which had rushed unerringly to its magnet. It is the knowledge that weakness will only arouse tenderness, never disgust, as when the fancy reigns and the heart sleeps; that faults will clothe themselves in the individuality of the owner and become treasures to the loving mind that sees, but worships. It is the development of the highest form of selfishness, the passionate and abiding desire to sacrifice one's self to the happiness of one beloved. Above all, it is the impossibility to cease to love, no matter what reason, or prudence, or jealousy, or disapproval, or terrible discoveries, may dictate. Let the mind sit on high and argue the soul's mate out of doors, it will rebound, when all is said and done, like a rubber ball when the pressure of the finger is removed. As for Chonita she is the lost part of me."

He left that day, and without seeing Chonita again. Valencia was in wildest delirium for a week; at the end of the second every hair on her head, her brows, and her eyelashes had fallen. She looked like a white mummy, a ghastly pitiful caricature of the beautiful woman whose arrows quivered in so many hearts. They rolled her in a blanket and took her home; and then I sought Chonita, who had barely left her room and never gone to Valencia's. I told her that I had witnessed the curse, and described the result.

"Have you no remorse?" I asked.

"None."

"You have ruined the beauty, the happiness, the fortune, of another woman."

"I have done what I intended."

"Do you realize that again you have raised a barrier between yourself and your religion? You do not look very repentant."

"Revenge is sweeter than religion."

Then in a burst of anger I confessed that I had told Estenega. For a moment I thought her terrible hatred was about to hurl its vengeance at me; but she only asked,—

"What did he say?"

Unwillingly, I repeated it, but word for word. And as I spoke, her face softened, the austerity left her features, an expression of passionate gratitude came into her eyes.

"Did he say that, Eustaquia?"

"He did."

"Say it again, please."

I did so. And then she put her hands to her face, and cried, and cried, and cried.

XXVII

At the end of the week Dona Trinidad died suddenly. She was sitting on the green bench, dispensing charities, when her head fell back gently, and the light went out. No death ever had been more peaceful, no soul ever had been better prepared; but wailing grief went after her. Poor Don Guillermo sank in a heap as if some one had felled him, Reinaldo wept loudly, and Prudencia was not to be consoled. Chonita was away on her horse when it happened, galloping over the hills. Servants were sent for her immediately, and met her when she was within an hour or two of home. As she entered the sala, Don Guillermo, Reinaldo, and Prudencia literally flung themselves upon her; and she stood like a rock, and supported them. She had loved her mother, but it had always been her lot to prop other people; she never had had a chance to lean.

All that night and next day she was closely engaged with the members of the agonized household, even visiting the grief-stricken Indians at times. On the second night she went to the room where her mother lay with all the pomp of candles and crosses, and bade the Indian watchers, crouching like buzzards about the corpse, to go for a time. She sank into a chair beside the dead, and wondered at the calmness of her heart. She was not conscious of any feeling stronger than regret. She tried to realize the irrevocableness of death,—that the mother who had been so kindly an influence in her life had gone out of it. But the knowledge brought no grief. She felt only the necessity for alleviating the grief of the others; that was her part.

The door opened. She drew her breath suddenly. She knew that it was Estenega. He sat down beside her and took her hand and held it, without a word, for hours. Gradually she leaned toward him, although without touching him. And after a time tears came.

He went his way the next morning, but he wrote to her before he left, and again from Monterey, and then from the North. She only answered once, and then with only a line.

But the line was this:

"Write to me until you have forgotten me."

One day she brought me a package and asked me to take it to Valencia. "It is an ointment," she said,—"one of old Brigida's" (a witch who lived on the cliffs and concocted wondrous specifics from herbs). "Tell her to use it and her hair will grow again."

And that was the only sign of penitence I was permitted to see.

Then for a long interval there came no word from Estenega.

XXVIII

Before going to Mexico, Estenega remained for some weeks at his ranchos in the North, overlooking the slaughtering of his cattle, an important yearly event, for the trade in hides and tallow with foreign shippers was the chief source of the Californian's income. He also was associated with the Russians at Fort Ross and Bodega in the fur-trade. But he was far from being satisfied with these desultory gains. They sufficed his private wants, but with the great schemes he had in mind he needed gold by the bushel. How to obtain it was a problem which sat on the throne of his mind side by side with Chonita Iturbi y Moncada. He had reason to believe that gold lay under California; but where? He determined that upon his return from Mexico he would take measures to discover, although he objected to the methods which alone could be employed. But, like all born rulers of men, he had an impatient scorn for means with a great end in view. There was no intermediate way of making the money. It would be a hundred years before the country would be populous enough to give his vast ranchos a reasonable value; and, although he had twenty thousand head of cattle, the market for their disposal was limited, and barter was the principle of trade, rather than coin.

Toward the end of the month he hurried to Monterey to catch a bark about to sail for Mexico. The important preliminaries of the future he had planned could no longer be delayed; the treacherous revengeful nature of Reinaldo might at any moment awake from the spell in which he had locked it; had a ship sailed before, he would have left his commercial interests with his mayor-domo and gone to the seat of government at once.

He arrived in Monterey one evening after hard riding. The city was singularly quiet. It was the hour when the indefatigable dancers of that gay town should have flitted past the open windows of the salas, when the air should have been vocal with the flute and guitar, song and light laughter. But the city might have been a living tomb. The white rayless houses were heavy and silent as sepulchers. He rode slowly down Alvarado Street, and saw the advancing glow of a cigar. When the cigar was abreast of him he recognized Mr. Larkin.

"What is the matter?" he asked.

"Small-pox," replied the consul, succinctly. "Better get on board at once. And steer clear of the lower quarter. Your vaquero arrived yesterday, and I instructed him to put your baggage in the custom-house. He dropped it and fled to the country."

Estenega thanked him and proceeded on his way. He made a circuit to avoid the lower quarter, but saw that it was not abandoned; lights moved here and there. "Poor creatures!" he thought, "they are probably dying like poisoned rats."

On the side of the hill by the road was a solitary hut. He was obliged to pass it. A candle burned beyond the open window, and he set his lips and turned his head; not from fear of contagion, however. And his eyes were drawn to the window in spite of his resolute will. He looked once, and looked again, then checked his horse. On the bed lay a girl in the middle stages of the disease, her eyes glittering with delirium, her black hair matted and wet. She was evidently alone. Estenega spurred his horse and galloped around to the back of the hut. In the kitchen, the only other room, huddled an old crone, brown and gnarled like an old apple. She was sleeping; by her side was a bottle of aguardiente. Estenega called loudly to her.

"Susana!"

The creature stirred, but did not open her eyes. He called twice again, and awakened her. She stared through the open door, her lower jaw falling, showing the yellow stumps.

"Who is?"

"Is Anita alone with you?"

"Ay, yi! Don Diego! Yes, yes. All run from the house like rats from a ship that burns. Ay, yi! Ay, yi! and she so pretty before! A-y, y-i!—" Her head fell forward; she relapsed into stupor.

Estenega rode around to the window again. The girl was sitting on the edge of the bed, mechanically pulling the long matted strands of her hair.

"Water! water!" she cried, faintly. "Ay, Mary!" She strove to rise, but fell back, clutching at the bedclothing.

Estenega rode to a deserted hut near by, concealed his saddle in a corner under a heap of rubbish, and turned his horse loose. He returned to the hut where the sick girl lay, and entered the room. She recognized him in spite of her fever.

"Don Diego! Is it you?—you?" she said, half raising herself. "Ay, Mary! is it the delirium?"

"It is I," he said. "I will take care of you. Do you want water?"

"Ay, water. Ay, thou wert always kind, even though thy love did last so little a while."

He brought the water and did what he could to relieve her sufferings: like all the rancheros, he had some knowledge of medicine. He held the old crone under the pump, gave her an emetic, broke her bottle, and ordered her to help him care for the girl. Between awe of him and promise of gold, she gave him some assistance.

Estenega watched the vessel sail the next morning, and battled with the impulse to leap from the window, hire a boat, and overtake it. The delay of a month might mean the death of his hopes. For all he knew, the bark carried the letters of his undoing; Reinaldo himself might be on it. He set his lips with an expression of bitter contempt—the expression directed at his own impotence in the hands of Circumstance,—and went to the bedside of the girl. She was hopelessly ill; even medical skill, were there such a thing in the country, could not save her; but he could not leave to die like a dog a woman who had been his mistress, even if only the fancy of a week, as this poor girl had been. She had loved him, and never annoyed him; they had maintained friendly relations, and he had helped her whenever she had appealed to him. But in this hour of her extremity she had further rights, and he recognized them. He had cut her hair close to her head, and she looked more comfortable, although an unpleasant sight. As he regarded her, he thought of Chonita, and the tide of love rose in him as it had not before. In the beginning he had been hardly more than infatuated with her originality and her curious beauty; at Santa Barbara her sweetness and kinship had stolen into him and the momentous fusion of passion and spiritual love had given new birth to a torpid soul and stirred and shaken his manhood as lust had never done; now in her absence and exaltation above common mortals he reverenced her as an ideal. Even in the bitterness of the knowledge that months must elapse before he could see her again, the tenderness she had drawn to herself from the serious depths of his nature throbbed throughout him, and made him more than gentle to the poor creature whose ignorance could not have comprehended the least of what he felt for Chonita.

She died within three days. The good priest, who stood to his post and made each of his afflicted poor a brief daily visit, prayed by her as she fell into stupor, but she was incapable of receiving extreme unction. Estenega was alone with her when she died, but the priest returned a few moments later.

"Don Thomas Larkin wishes me to say to you, Don Diego Estenega," said the Father, "that he would be glad to have you stay with him until the next vessel arrives. As two members of his family have the disease, he has nothing to fear from you. I will care for the body."

Estenega handed him money for the burial, and looked at him speculatively. The priest must have heard the girl's confessions, and he wondered why he did not improve the opportunity to reprove a man whose indifference to the Church was a matter of indignant comment among the clergy. The priest appeared to divine his thoughts, for he said:

"Thou hast done more than thy duty, Don Diego. And to the frailties of men I think the good God is merciful. He made them. Go in peace."

Estenega accepted Mr. Larkin's invitation, but, in spite of the genial society of the consul, he spent in his house the most wretched three weeks of his life. He dared not leave Monterey until he had passed the time of incubation, having no desire to spread the disease; he dared not write to Chonita, for the same reason. What must she think? She supposed him to have sailed, of course, but he had promised to write her from Monterey, and again from San Diego. And the uncertainty regarding his Mexican affairs was intolerable to a man of his active mind and supertense nervous system. His only comfort lay in Mr. Larkin's assurance that the national bark Joven Guipuzcoana was due within the month and would return at once. Early in the fourth week the assurance was fulfilled, and by the time he was ready to sail again his danger from contagion was over. But he embarked without writing to Chonita.

The voyage lasted a month, tedious and monotonous, more trying than his retardation on land, for there at least he could recover some serenity by violent exercise. He divided his time between pacing the deck, when the weather permitted, and writing to Chonita: long, intimate, possessing letters, which would reveal her to herself as nothing else, short of his own dominant contact, could do. At San Blas he posted his letters and welcomed the rough journey overland to the capital; but under a calm exterior he was possessed of the spirit of disquiet. As so often happens, however, his fears proved to have been vagaries of a morbid state of mind and of that habit of thought which would associate with every cause an effect of similar magnitude. Santa Ana welcomed him with friendly enthusiasm, and was ready to listen to his plans. That wily and astute politician, who was always abreast of progress and never in its lead, recognized in Estenega the coming man, and, knowing that the seizure of the Californias by the United States was only a question of time, was keenly willing to make an ally of the man who he foresaw would control them as long as he chose, both at home and in Washington. For the matter of that, he recognized the impotence of Mexico to interfere, beyond bluster, with plans any resolute Californian might choose to pursue; but it was important to Estenega's purpose that the governorship should be assured to him by the central government, and the eyes of the Mexican Congress directed elsewhere. He knew the value of the moral effect which its apparent sanction would have upon rebellious Southerners.

"I am at your service," said Santa Ana; "and the governorship is yours. But take heed that no rumor of your ultimate intentions reaches the ears of Congress until you are firmly established. If it opposed you relentlessly—and it keeps its teeth on California like a dog on a bone bigger than himself—I should have to yield; I have too much at stake myself. I will look out that any communications from enemies, including Iturbi y Moncada, are opened first by me."

Estenega wrote to Chonita again by the ship that left during his brief stay in the capital, and it was his intention to go directly to Santa Barbara upon arriving in California. But when he landed in Monterey—disinfected and careless as of old—he learned that she was about to start, perhaps already had done so, for Fort Ross, to pay a visit to the Rotscheffs. The news gave him pleasure; it had been his wish to say what he had yet to say in his own forests.

And then the plan which had been stirring restlessly in his mind for many months took imperative shape: he determined that if there was gold in California he would wring the secret out of its keeper, by gentle means or violent, and that within the next twenty-four hours.

XXIX

Estenega drew rein the next night before the neglected Mission of San Rafael. The valley, surrounded by hills dark with the silent redwoods, bore not a trace of the populous life of the days before secularization. The padre lived alone, lodge-keeper of a valley of shadows.

He opened the door of his room on the corridor as he heard the approach of the traveler, squinting his bleared, yellow-spotted eyes. He was surly by nature, but he bowed low to the man whose power was so great in California, and whose generosity had sent him many a bullock. He cooked him supper from his frugal store, piled the logs in the open fireplace,—November was come,—and, after a bottle of wine, produced from Estenega's saddle-bag, expanded into a hermit's imitation of conviviality. Late in the night they still sat on either side of the table in the dusty, desolate room. The Forgotten had been entertained with vivid and shifting pictures of the great capital in which he had passed his boyhood. He smiled occasionally; now and again he gave a quick impatient sigh. Suddenly Estenega leaned forward and fixed him with his powerful gaze.

"Is there gold in these mountains?" he asked, abruptly.

The priest was thrown off his guard for a moment; a look of

Gertrude Franklin Horn Atherton

meaning flashed into his eyes, then one of cunning displaced it.

"It may be, Senor Don Diego; gold is often in the earth. But had I the unholy knowledge, I would lock it in my breast. Gold is the canker in the heart of the world. It is not for the Church to scatter the evil broadcast."

Estenega shut his teeth. Fanaticism was a more powerful combatant than avarice.

"True, my father. But think of the good that gold has wrought. Could these Missions have been built without gold?—these thousands of Indians Christianized?"

"What you say is not untrue; but for one good, ten thousand evils are wrought with the metal which the devil mixed in hell and poured through the veins of the earth."

Estenega spent a half-hour representing in concrete and forcible images the debt which civilization owed to the fact and circulation of gold. The priest replied that California was a proof that commerce could exist by barter; the money in the country was not worth speaking of.

"And no progress to speak of in a hundred years," retorted Estenega. Then he expatiated upon the unique future of California did she have gold to develop her wonderful resources. The priest said that to cut California from her Arcadian simplicity would be to start her on her journey to the devil along with the corrupt nations of the Old World. Estenega demonstrated that if there was vice in the older civilizations there was also a higher state of mental development, and that Religion held her own. He might as well have addressed the walls of the Mission. He tempted with the bait of one of the more central Missions. The priest had only the dust of ambition in the cellar of his brain.

He lost his patience at last. "I must have gold," he said, shortly; "and you shall show me where to find it. You once betrayed to my father that you knew of its existence in these hills; and you shall give me the key."

The priest looked into the eyes of steel and contemptuously determined face before him, and shut his lips. He was alone with a desperate man; he had not even a servant; he could be murdered, and his murderer go unsuspected; but the heart of the fanatic was in him. He made no reply.

"You know me," said Estenega. "I owe half my power in California to the fact that I do not make a threat to-day and forget it to-morrow. You will show me where that gold is, or I shall kill you."

"The servant of God dies when his hour comes. If I am to die by the hand of the assassin, so be it."

Estenega leaned forward and placed his strong hand about the priest's baggy throat, pushing the table against his chest. He pressed his thumb against the throttle, his second finger hard against the jugular, and the tongue rolled over the teeth, the congested eyes bulged. "It may be that you scorn death, but may not fancy the mode of it. I have no desire to kill you. Alive or dead, your life is of no more value than that of a worm. But you shall die, and die with much discomfort, unless you do as I wish." His hand relaxed its grasp, but still pressed the rough dirty throat.

"Accursed heretic!" said the priest.

"Spare your curses for the superstitious."

He saw a gleam of cunning come into the priest's eyes. "Very well; if I must I must. Let me rise, and I will conduct you."

Estenega took a piece of rope from his saddle-bag and tied it about the priest's waist and his own. "If you have any holy pitfall in view for me, I shall have the pleasure of your company. And if I am led into labyrinths to die of starvation, you at least will have a meal: I could not eat you."

If the priest was disconcerted, he did not show it. He took a lantern from a shelf, lit the fragment of candle, and, opening a door at the back, walked through the long line of inner rooms. All were heaped with rubbish. In one he found a trap-door with his foot, and descended rough steps cut out of the earth. The air rose chill and damp, and Estenega knew that the tunnel of the Mission was below, the secret exit to the hills which the early Fathers built as a last resource in case of defeat by savage tribes. When they reached the bottom of the steps the tallow dip illuminated but a narrow circle; Estenega could form no idea of the workmanship of the tunnel, except that it was not more than six feet and a few inches high, for his hat brushed the top, and that the floor and sides appeared to be of pressed clay. There was ventilation somewhere, but no light. They walked a mile or more, and then Estenega had a sense of stepping into a wider and higher excavation.

"We are no longer in the tunnel," said the priest. He lifted the lantern and swung it above his head. Estenega saw that they were in a circular room, hollowed probably out of the heart of a hill. He also saw something else.

"What is that?" he exclaimed, sharply.

The priest handed him the lantern. "Look for yourself," he said.

Estenega took the lantern, and, holding it just above his head and close to the walls, slowly traversed the room. It was belted with three strata of crystal-like quartz, sown thick with glittering yellow specks and chunks. Each stratum was about three feet wide.

"There is a fortune here," he said. He felt none of the greed of gold, merely a recognition of its power.

"Yes, senor; enough to pay the debt of a nation."

"Where are we? Under what hill? I am sorry I had not a compass with me. It was impossible to make any accurate guess of direction in that slanting tunnel. Where is the outlet?"

The priest made no reply.

Estenega turned to him peremptorily. "Answer me. How can I find this place from without?"

"You never will find it from without. When the danger from Indians was over, a pious Father closed the opening. This gold is not for you. You could not find even the trap-door by yourself."

"Then why have you brought me here?"

"To tantalize you. To punish you for your insult to the Church through me. Kill me now, if you wish. Better death than hell."

Estenega made a rapid circuit of the room. There was no mode of egress other than that by which they had entered, and no sign of any previously existing. He sprang upon the priest and shook him until the worn stumps rattled in their gums. "You dog!" he said, "to balk me with your ignorant superstition! Take me out of this place by its other entrance at once, that I may remain on the hill until morning. I would not trust your word. You shall tell me, if I have to torture you."

The priest made a sudden spring and closed with Estenega, hugging him like a bear. The lantern fell and went out. The two men stumbled blindly in the blackness, striking the walls, wrestling desperately, the priest using his teeth and panting like a beast. But he was no match for the virility and science of his young opponent. Estenega threw him in a moment and bound him with the rope. Then he found the lantern and lit the candle again. He returned to the priest and stood over him. The latter was conquered physically, but the dogged light of bigotry still burned in his eyes, although Estenega's were not agreeable to face.

Estenega was furious. He had twisted Santa Ana, one of the most subtle and self-seeking men of his time, around his finger as if he had been a yard of ribbon; Alvarado, the wisest man ever born in the Californias, was swayed by his judgment; yet all the arts of which his intellect was master fell blunt and useless before this clay-brained priest. He had more respect for the dogs in his kennels, but unless he resorted to extreme measures the creature would defeat him through sheer brute ignorance. Estenega was not a man to stop in sight of victory or to give his sword to an enemy he despised.

"You are at my mercy. You realize that now, I suppose. Will you show me the other way out?"

The priest drew down his under-lip like a snarling dog, revealing the discolored stumps. But he made no other reply.

Estenega lit a match, and, kneeling beside the priest, held it to his stubbled beard. As the flame licked the flesh the man uttered a yell like a kicked brute. Estenega sprang to his feet with an oath. "I can't do it!" he exclaimed, with bitter disgust. "I haven't the iron of cruelty in me. I am not fit to be a ruler of men." He untied the rope about the prisoner's feet. "Get up," he said, "and conduct me back as we came." The priest scrambled to his feet and hobbled down the long tunnel. They ascended the steps beneath the Mission and emerged into the room. Estenega turned swiftly to prevent the closing of the trap-door, but only in time to hear it shut with a spring and the priest kick rubbish above it.

He cut the rope which bound the other's hands. "Go," he said, "I have no further use for you. And if you report this, I need not explain to you that it will fare worse with you than it will with me."

The priest fled, and Estenega, hanging the lantern on a nail, pushed aside the rubbish with his feet, purposing to pace the room until dawn. In a few moments, however, he discovered that the despised hermit was not without his allies; ten thousand fleas, the pest of the country, assaulted every portion of his body they could reach. They swarmed down the legs of his riding-boots, up his trousers, up his sleeves, down his neck. "There is no such thing in life as tragedy," he thought. He hung the lantern outside the door to mark the room, and paced the yard until morning. But there were dark hours yet before the dawn, and during one of them a figure, when his back was turned, crept to the lantern and hung it before an adjoining room. When light came,—and the fog came first,—all Estenega's efforts to find the trap-door were unavailing, although the yard was littered with the rubbish he flung into it from the room. He suspected the trick, but there were ten rooms exactly alike, and although he cleared most of them he could discover no trace of the trap-door. He looked at the hills surrounding the Mission. They were many, and beyond there were others. He mounted his horse and rode around the buildings, listening carefully for hollow reverberation. The tunnel was too far below; he heard nothing.

He was defeated. For the first time in his life he was without resource, overwhelmed by a force stronger than his own will; and his spirit was savage within him. He had no authority to dig the floors of the Mission, for the Mission and several acres about it were the property of the Church. The priest never would take him on that underground journey again, for he had learned the weak spot in his armor, nor had he fear of death. Unless accident favored him, or some one more fortunate, the golden heart of the San Rafael hill would pulse unrifled forever.

XXX

He turned his back upon the Mission and rode toward his home, sixty miles in a howling November wind. At Bodega Bay he learned that Governor Rotscheff had passed there two days before with a party of guests that he had gone down to Sausalito to meet. Chonita awaited him in the North. A softer mood pressed through the somberness of his spirit, and the candle of hope burned again. Gold must exist elsewhere in California, and he swore anew that it should yield itself to him. The last miles of his ride lay along the cliffs. Sometimes the steep hills covered with redwoods rose so abruptly from the trail that the undergrowth brushed him as he passed; on the other side but a few inches stood between himself and death amidst the surf pounding on the rocks a thousand feet below. The sea-gulls screamed about his head, the sea-lions barked with the hollow note of consumptives on the outlying rocks. On the horizon was a bank of fog, outlined with the crests and slopes and gulches of the mountain beside him. It sent an advance wrack scudding gracefully across the ocean to puff among the redwoods, capriciously clinging to some, ignoring others. Then came the vast white mountain rushing over the roaring ocean, up the cliffs and into the gloomy forests, blotting the lonely horseman from sight.

He arrived at his house—a big structure of logs—late in the

night. His servants came out to meet him, and in a moment a fire leaped in the great fireplace in his library. He lived alone; his parents and brothers were dead, and his sisters married; but the fire made the low long room, covered with bear-skins and lined with books, as cheerful as a bachelor could expect. He found a note from the Princess Helene Rotscheff, the famous wife of the governor, asking him to spend the following week at Fort Ross; but he was so tired that even the image of Chonita was dim; the note barely caused a throb of anticipation. After supper he flung himself on a couch before the fire and slept until morning, then went to bed and slept until afternoon. By that time he was himself again. He sent a vaquero ahead with his evening clothes, and an hour or two later started for Fort Ross, spurring his horse with a lighter heart over the cliffs. His ranchos adjoined the Russian settlement; the journey from his house to the military enclosure was not a long one. He soon rounded the point of a sloping hill and entered the spreading core formed by the mountains receding in a semicircle above the cliffs, and in whose shelter lay Fort Ross. The fort was surrounded by a stockade of redwood beams, bastions in the shape of hexagonal towers at diagonal corners. Cannon, mounted on carriages, were at each of the four entrances, in the middle of the enclosure, and in the bastions. Sentries paced the ramparts with unremitting vigilance.

Within were the long low buildings occupied by the governor and officers, the barracks, and the Russian church, with its belfry and cupola. Beyond was the "town," a collection of huts accommodating about eight hundred Indians and Siberian convicts, the workingmen of the company. All the buildings were of redwood logs or planed boards, and made a very different picture from the white towns of the South. The curving mountains were sombrous with redwoods, the ocean growled unceasingly.

Estenega threw his bridle to a soldier and went directly to the house. A servant met him on the veranda and conducted him to his room; it was late, and every one else was dressing for dinner. He changed his riding-clothes for the evening dress of modern civilization, and went at once to the drawing-room. Here all was luxury, nothing to suggest the privations of a new country. A thick red carpet covered the floor, red arras the walls; the music of Mozart and Beethoven was on the grand piano. The furniture was rich and comfortable, the large carved table was covered with French novels and European periodicals.

The candles had not been brought in, but logs blazed in the open fireplace. As Estenega crossed the room, a woman, dressed in black, rose from a deep chair, and he recognized Chonita. He sprang forward impetuously and held out his arms, but she waved him back.

"No, no," she said, hurriedly. "I want to explain why I am here. I came for two reasons. First, I could refuse the Princess Helene no longer; she goes so soon. And then—I wanted to see you once more before I leave the world."

"Before you do what?"

"I am not going into a convent; I cannot leave my father. I am going to retire to the most secluded of our ranchos, to see no more of the world or its people. I shall take my father with me. Reinaldo and Prudencia will remain at Casa Grande."

"Nonsense!" he exclaimed, impatiently. "Do you suppose I shall let you do anything of the sort? How little you know me, my love! But we will discuss that question later. We shall be alone only a few moments now. Tell me of yourself. How are you?"

"I will tell you that, also, at another time."

And at the moment a door opened, and the governor and his wife entered and greeted Estenega with cordial hospitality. The governor was a fine-looking Russian, with a spontaneous warmth of manner; the princess a woman who possessed both elegance and vivacity, both coquetry and dignity; she could sparkle and chill, allure and suppress in the same moment. Even here, rough and wild as her surroundings were, she gave much thought to her dress; to-night her blonde harmonious loveliness was properly framed in a toilette of mignonette greens, fresh from Paris. A moment later Reinaldo and Prudencia appeared, the former as splendid a caballero as ever, although wearing the chastened air of matrimony, the latter pre-maternally consequential. Then came the officers and their wives, all brilliant in evening dress; and a moment later dinner was announced.

Estenega sat at the right of his hostess, and that trained daughter of the salon kept the table in a light ripple of conversation, sparkling herself, without striking terror to the hearts of her guests. She and Estenega were old friends, and usually indulged in lively sallies, ending some times in a sharp war of words, for she was a very clever woman; but to-night he gave her absent attention: he watched Chonita furtively, and thought of little else.

Her eyes had darker shadows beneath them than those cast by her lashes; her face was pale and slightly hollowed. She had suffered, and not for her mother. "She shall suffer no more," he thought.

"We hunt bear to-night," he heard the governor say at length.

"I should like to go," said Chonita, quickly. "I should like to go out to-night."

Immediately there was a chorus from all the Other women, excepting the Princess Helene and Prudencia; they wanted to go too. Rotscheff, who would much rather have left them at home, consented with good grace, and Estenega's spirits rose at once. He would have a talk with Chonita that night, something he had not dared to hope for, and he suspected that she had promoted the opportunity.

The men remained in the dining-room after the ladies had withdrawn, and Estenega, restored to his normal condition, and in his natural element among these people of the world, expanded into the high spirits and convivial interest in masculine society which made him as popular with men as he was fascinating, through the exercise of more subtle faculties, to women. Reinaldo watched him with jealous impatience; no one cared to hearken to his eloquence when Estenega talked; and he had come to Fort Ross only to have a conversation with his one-time enemy. As he listened to Estenega, shorn, for the time-being, of his air of dictator and watchful ambition, a man of the world taking an enthusiastic part in the hilarity of the hour, but never sacrificing his dignity by assuming the role of chief entertainer, there grew within him a dull sense of inferiority: he felt, rather than knew, that neither the city of Mexico nor gratified ambitions would give him that assured ease, that perfection of breeding, that calm sense of power, concealing so gracefully the relentless will and the infinite resource which made this most un-Californian of Californians seem to his Arcadian eyes a being of a higher star. And hatred blazed forth anew.

As the men rose, finally, to go to the drawing-room, he asked Estenega to remain for a moment. "Thou wilt keep thy promise soon, no?" he said when they were alone.

"What promise?"

"Thy promise to send me as diputado to the next Mexican Congress."

Estenega looked at him reflectively. He had little toleration for the man of inferior brain, and, although he did not underrate his power for mischief, he relied upon his own wit to circumvent him. He had disposed of this one by warning Santa Ana, and he concluded to be annoyed by him no further. Besides, as a brother-in-law, he would be insupportable except at the long range of mutual unamiability.

"I made you no promise," he said, deliberately; "and I shall make you none. I do not wish you in the city of Mexico."

Reinaldo's face grew livid. "Thou darest to say that to me, and yet would marry my sister?"

"I would, and I shall."

"And yet thou wouldst not help her brother?"

"Her brother is less to me than any man with whom I have sat to-night. Build no hopes on that. You will stay at Santa Barbara and play the grand seigneur, which suits you very well, or become a prisoner in your own house." And he left the room.

XXXI

An hour later they assembled in the plaza to start for the bear hunt. Reinaldo was not of the party.

Estenega lifted Chonita to her horse and stood beside her for a moment while the others mounted. He touched her hand with his:

"We could not have a more beautiful night," he said, significantly. "And I have often wished that my father had included this spot when he applied for his grant. I should like to live with you here. Even when the winds rage and hurl the rain through the very window pane, I know of no more enchanting spot than Fort Ross. The Russians are going; some day I will buy it for you."

She made no reply, but she did not withdraw her hand, and he held it closely and glanced slowly about him. Always, despite his bitter intimacy with life, in kinship with nature, perhaps in that moment it had a deeper meaning, for he saw with double vision: She was there; and, with him, sensible not only of the beauty of the night, but of the indefinable mystery which broods over California the moment the sun falls. Perhaps, too, he was troubled by a vague foreboding, such as comes to mortals sometimes in spite of their limitations: he never saw Fort Ross again.

On the horizon the fog crouched and moved; marched like a battalion of ocean's ghosts; suddenly cohered and sent out light puffs of smoke, as from the crater of a spectral volcano. The moon, full and bright and cold, hung low in the dark sky: one hardly noted the stars. The vast sweep of water was as calm as a lake, dark and metallic like the sky, barely reflecting the silver light between. But although calm it was not quiet. It greeted the forbidding rocks beyond the shore, the long irregular line of stark, storm-beaten cliffs, with ominous mutter, now and again throwing a cloud of spray high in the air, as if in derisive proof that even in sleep it was sensible of its power. Occasionally it moaned, as if sounding a dirge along the mass of stones which storms had hurled or waves had wrenched from the crags above,—a dirge for beheaded Russians, for him who had walked the plank, or for the lover of Natalie Ivanhoff.

Here and there the cliffs were intersected by deep straggling gulches, out of whose sides grew low woods of brush; but the three tables rising successively from the ocean to the forest on the mountain, were almost bare. On the highest, between two gulches, on a knoll so bare and black and isolated that its destiny was surely taken into account at creation, was a tall rude cross and a half hundred neglected graves. The forest seemed blacker just behind it, the shadows thicker in the gorges that embraced it, the ocean grayer and more illimitable before it. "Natalie Ivanhoff is there in her copper coffin," said Estenega, "forgotten already."

The curve of the mountain was so perfect that it seemed to reach down a long arm on either side and grasp the cliffs. The redwoods on its crown and upper slopes were a mass of rigid shadows, the points, only, sharply etched on the night sky. They might have been a wall about an undiscovered country.

"Come," cried Rotscheff, "we are ready to start." And Estenega sprang to his horse.

"I don't envy you," said the Princess Helene from the veranda, her silveren head barely visible above the furs which enveloped her. "I prefer the fire."

"You are warmly clad?" asked Estenega of Chonita. "But you have the blood of the South in your veins."

They climbed the steep road between the levels, slowly, the women chattering and asking questions, the men explaining and advising. Estenega and Chonita having much to say, said nothing.

A cold volume of air, the muffled roar of a mountain torrent, rushed out of the forest, startling with the suddenness of its impact. Once a panther uttered its human cry.

They entered the forest. It was so dark here that the horses wandered from the trail and into the brush again and again. Conversation ceased; except for the muffled footfalls of the horses and the speech of the waters there was no sound. Chonita had never known a stillness so profound; the giant trees crowding together seemed to resent intrusion, to menace an eternal silence. She moved her horse close to Estenega's and he took her hand. Occasionally there was an opening, a well of blackness, for the moon had not yet come to the forest.

They reached the summit, and descended. Half-way down the mountain they rode into a farm in a valley formed by one of the many basins.

The Indians were waiting, and killed a bullock at once, placing the carcass in a conspicuous place. Then all retired to the shade of the trees. In less than a half-hour a bear came prowling out of the forest and began upon the meal so considerately provided for him. When his attention was fully engaged, Rotscheff and the officers, mounted, dashed down upon him, swinging their lassos. The bear showed fight and stood his ground, but this was an occasion when the bear always got the worst of it. One lasso caught his neck, another his hind foot, and he was speedily strained and strangled to death. No sooner was he despatched than another appeared, then another, and the sport grew very exciting, absorbing the attention of the women as well as the energies of the men.

Estenega lifted Chonita from her horse. "Let us walk," he said. "They will not miss us. A few yards farther, and you will be on my territory. I want you there."

She made no protest, and they entered the forest. The moon shone down through the lofty redwoods that seemed to scrape its crystal; the monotone of the distant sea blended with the faint roar of the tree-tops. The vast gloomy aisles were unbroken by other sound.

He took her hand and held it a moment, then drew it through his arm. "Now tell me all," he said, "They will be occupied for a long while. The night is ours."

"I have come here to tell you that I love you," she said. "Ah, can *I* make *you* tremble? It was impossible for me not to tell you this; I could not rest in my retreat without having the last word with you, without having you know me. And I want to tell you that I have suffered horribly; you may care to know that, for no one else in the world could have made me, no one else ever can. Only your fingers could twist in my heart-strings and tear my heart out of my body. I suffered first because I doubted you, then because I loved you, then the torture of jealousy and the pangs of parting, then those dreadful three months when I heard no word. I could not stay at Casa Grande; everything associated with you drove me wild. Oh, I have gone through all varieties! But the last was the worst, after I heard from you again, and all other causes were removed, and I knew that you were well and still loved me: the knowledge that I never could be anything to you,—and I could be so much! The torment of this knowledge was so bitter that there was but one refuge,—imagination. I shut my eyes to my little world and lived with you; and it seemed to me that I grew into absolute knowledge of you. Let me tell you what I divined. You may tell me that I am wrong, but I do not believe that you will. I think that in the little time we were together I absorbed you.

"It seemed to me that your soul reached always for something just above the attainable, restless in the moments which would satisfy another, fretted with a perverse desire for something different when an ardent wish was granted, steeped, under all wanton determined enjoyment of life, with the bitter knowing of life's sure impotence to satisfy. Could the dissatisfied darting mind loiter long enough to give a woman more than the promise of happiness?—but never mind that.

"With this knowledge of you my own resistless desire for variety left me: my nature concentrated into one paramount wish,—to be all things to you. What I had felt vaguely before and stifled—the nothingness of life, the inevitableness of satiety—I repudiated utterly, now that they were personified in you; I would not recognize the fact of their existence. *I* could make you happy. How could imagination shape such scenes, such perfection of union, of companionship, if reality were not? Imagination is the child of inherited and living impressions. I might exaggerate; but, even stripped of its halo, the substance must be sweeter and more fulfilling than anything else on this earth at least. And I knew that you loved me. Oh, I had *felt* that! And the variousness of your nature and desires, although they might madden me at times, would give an extraordinary zest to life. I was The Doomswoman no longer. I was a supplementary being who could meet you in every mood and complete it; who would so understand that I could be man and woman and friend to you. A delusion? But so long as I shall never know, let me believe. An extraordinary tumultuous desire that rose in me like a wave and shook me often at first, had, in those last sad weeks, less part in my musings. It seemed to me that that was the expression, the poignant essence, of love; but there was so much else! I do not understand that, however, and never shall. But I wanted to tell you all. I could not rest until you knew me as I am and as you had made me. And I will tell you this too," she cried, breaking suddenly, "I wanted you so! Oh, I needed you so! It was not I, only, who could give. And it is so terrible for a woman to stand alone!"

He made no reply for a moment. But he forgot every other interest and scheme and idea stored in his impatient brain. He was thrilled to his soul, and filled with the exultant sense that he was about to take to his heart the woman compounded for him out of his own elements.

"Speak to me," she said.

"My love, I have so much to say to you that it will take all the years we shall spend together to say it in."

"No, no! Do not speak of that. There I am firm. Although the misery of the past months were to be multiplied ten hundred times in the future, I would not marry you."

Estenega, knowing that their hour of destiny was come, and that upon him alone depended its issues, was not the man to hesitate between such happiness as this woman alone could give him, and the gray existence which she in her blindness would have meted to both: his bold will had already taken the future in its relentless grasp. But, knowing the mental habit of women, he thought it best to let Chonita free her mind, that there might be the less in it to protest for hearing while his heart and passion spoke to hers.

"It seems absurd to argue the matter," he said, "but tell me the reasons again, if you choose, and we will dispose of them once for all. Do not think for a moment, my darling, that I do not respect your reasons; but I respect them only because they are yours; in themselves they are not worthy of consideration."

"Ay, but they are. It has been an unwritten law for four generations that an Estenega and an Iturbi y Moncada should not marry; the enmity began, as you should know, when a member of each family was an officer in a detachment of troops sent to protect the Missions in their building. And my father—he told me lately—loved your father's sister for many years,—that was the reason he married so late in life,—and would not ask her because of her blood and of cruel wrongs her father had done his. Shall his daughter be weak where he was strong? You cast aside traditions as if they were the seeds of an apple; but remember that they are blood of my blood. And the vow I made,—do you forget that? And the words of it? The Church stands between us. I will tell you all: the priest has forbidden me to marry you; he forbade it every time I confessed; not only because of my vow, but because you had aroused in me a love so terrible that I almost took the life of another woman. Could I bring you back to the Church it might be different; but you rule others; no one could remould you. You see it is hopeless. It is no use to argue."

"I have no intention of arguing. Words are too good to waste

Gertrude Franklin Horn Atherton

on such an absurd proposition that because our fathers hated, we, who are independent and intelligent beings, should not marry when every drop of heart's blood demands its rights. As for your vow,—what is a vow? Hysterical egotism, nothing more. Were it the promise of man to man, the subject would be worth discussing. But we will settle the matter in our own way." He took her suddenly in his arms and kissed her. She put her arms about him and clung to him, trembling, her lips pressed to his. In that supreme moment he felt not happiness, but a bitter desire to bear her out of the world into some higher sphere where the conditions of happiness might possibly exist. "On the highest pinnacle we reach," he thought, "we are granted the tormenting and chastening glimpse of what might be, had God, when he compounded his victims, been in a generous mood and completed them."

And she? she was a woman.

"You will resist no longer," he said, in a few moments.

"Ay, more surely than ever, now." Her voice was faint, but crossed by a note of terror. "In that moment I forgot my religion and my duty. And what is so sweet,—it cannot be right."

"Do you so despise your womanhood, the most perfect thing about you?"

"Oh, let us return! I wanted to kiss you once. I meant to do that. But I should not—Let us go! Oh, I love you so! I love you so!"

He drew her closer and kissed her until her head fell forward and her body grew heavy. "I shall think and act now, for both," he said, unsteadily, although there was no lack of decision in his voice. "You are mine. I claim you, and I shall run no further risk of losing you. Oh, you will forgive me—my love—"

Neither saw a man walking rapidly up the trail. Suddenly the man gave a bound and ran toward them. It was Reinaldo.

"Ah, I have found thee," he cried. "Listen, Don Diego Estenega, lord of the North, American, and would-be dictator of the Californias. Two hours ago I despatched a vaquero with a circular letter to the priests of the Department of the Californias, warning them each and all to write at once to the Archbishop of Mexico, and protest that the success of your ambitions would mean the downfall of the Catholic Church in California, and telling them your schemes. Thou art mighty, O Don Diego Estenega, but thou art powerless against the enmity of the Church. They are mightier than thou, and thou wilt never rule in California. Unhand my sister! Thou shalt not have her either. Thou shalt have nothing. Wilt thou unhand her?" he cried, enraged at Estenega's cold reception of his damnatory news. "Thou shouldst not have her if I tore thy heart from thy body."

Estenega looked contemptuously across Chonita's shoulder, although his heart was lead within him. "The last resource of the mean and down-trodden is revenge," he said. "Go. To-morrow I shall horsewhip you in the court-yard of Fort Ross."

Reinaldo, hot with excitement and thirst for further vengeance, uttered a shriek of rage and sprang upon him. Estenega saw the gleam of a knife and flung Chonita aside, catching the driving arm, the fury of his heart in his muscles. Reinaldo had the soft muscles of the cabellero, and panted and writhed in the iron grasp of the man who forgot that he grappled with the brother of a woman passionately loved, remembered only that he rejoiced to fight to the death the man who had ruined his life. Reinaldo tried to thrust the knife into his back; Estenega suddenly threw his weight on the arm that held it, nearly wrenching it from its socket, snatched the knife, and drove it to the heart of his enemy.

Then the hot blood in his body turned cold. He stood like a stone regarding Chonita, whose eyes, fixed upon him, were expanded with horror. Between them lay the dead body of her brother.

He turned with a groan and sat down on a fallen log, supporting his chin with his hand. His profile looked grim and worn and old. He stared unseeingly at the ground. Chonita stood, still looking at him. The last act of her brother's life had been to lay the foundation of her lover's ruin; his death had completed it: all the South would rise did the slayer of an Iturbi y Moncada seek to rule it. She felt vaguely sorry for Reinaldo; but death was peace; this was hell in living veins. The memory of the world beyond the forest grew indistinct. She recalled her first dream and turned in loathing from the bloodless selfishness of which it was the allegory. Superstition and tradition slipped into some inner pocket of her memory, there to rattle their dry bones together and fall to dust. She saw only the figure, relaxed for the first time, the profile of a man with his head on the block. She stepped across the body of her brother, and, kneeling beside Estenega, drew his head to her breast.

ABOUT THE AUTHOR

Gertrude Franklin Horn Atherton (October 30, 1857 – June 14, 1948) was an American writer.

She was born in San Francisco and lived in California all her life. She eloped with George H.B. Atherton when she was only 19, and had two children. Her husband discouraged her writing; and the serial publication of her first novel, The Randolphs of Redwoods (1882), though unsigned, scandalized her family.

After her husband's death, in 1887, she was free to pursue her writing career as a protégé of Ambrose Bierce, eventually writing 60 books and numerous articles. Atherton's first signed novel, What Dreams May Come, was published in 1888 under the pseudonym Frank Lin.

Her novels often feature strong heroines who pursue independent lives, undoubtedly a reaction to her stifling married life. She is best remembered for a series of historical novels and short stories set in California, including The Splendid, Idle Forties (1902); The Conqueror (1902), which is a fictionalized biography of Alexander Hamilton; and her sensational, semi-autobiographical novel Black Oxen (1923), about a middle-aged woman who miraculously becomes young again after glandular therapy.

Choose from Thousands of 1stWorldLibrary Classics By

A. M. Barnard
Ada Leverson
Adolphus William Ward
Aesop
Agatha Christie
Alexander Aaronsohn
Alexander Kielland
Alexandre Dumas
Alfred Gatty
Alfred Ollivant
Alice Duer Miller
Alice Turner Curtis
Alice Dunbar
Allen Chapman
Alleyne Ireland
Ambrose Bierce
Amelia E. Barr
Amory H. Bradford
Andrew Lang
Andrew McFarland Davis
Andy Adams
Angela Brazil
Anna Alice Chapin
Anna Sewell
Annie Besant
Annie Hamilton Donnell
Annie Payson Call
Annie Roe Carr
Annonaymous
Anton Chekhov
Archibald Lee Fletcher
Arnold Bennett
Arthur C. Benson
Arthur Conan Doyle
Arthur M. Winfield
Arthur Ransome
Arthur Schnitzler
Arthur Train
Atticus
B.H. Baden-Powell
B. M. Bower
B. C. Chatterjee
Baroness Emmuska Orczy
Baroness Orczy
Basil King
Bayard Taylor
Ben Macomber
Bertha Muzzy Bower
Bjornstjerne Bjornson

Booth Tarkington
Boyd Cable
Bram Stoker
C. Collodi
C. E. Orr
C. M. Ingleby
Carolyn Wells
Catherine Parr Traill
Charles A. Eastman
Charles Amory Beach
Charles Dickens
Charles Dudley Warner
Charles Farrar Browne
Charles Ives
Charles Kingsley
Charles Klein
Charles Hanson Towne
Charles Lathrop Pack
Charles Romyn Dake
Charles Whibley
Charles Willing Beale
Charlotte M. Braeme
Charlotte M. Yonge
Charlotte Perkins Stetson
Clair W. Hayes
Clarence Day Jr.
Clarence E. Mulford
Clemence Housman
Confucius
Coningsby Dawson
Cornelis DeWitt Wilcox
Cyril Burleigh
D. H. Lawrence
Daniel Defoe
David Garnett
Dinah Craik
Don Carlos Janes
Donald Keyhoe
Dorothy Kilner
Dougan Clark
Douglas Fairbanks
E. Nesbit
E. P. Roe
E. Phillips Oppenheim
E. S. Brooks
Earl Barnes
Edgar Rice Burroughs
Edith Van Dyne
Edith Wharton

Edward Everett Hale
Edward J. O'Biren
Edward S. Ellis
Edwin L. Arnold
Eleanor Atkins
Eleanor Hallowell Abbott
Eliot Gregory
Elizabeth Gaskell
Elizabeth McCracken
Elizabeth Von Arnim
Ellem Key
Emerson Hough
Emilie F. Carlen
Emily Bronte
Emily Dickinson
Enid Bagnold
Enilor Macartney Lane
Erasmus W. Jones
Ernie Howard Pie
Ethel May Dell
Ethel Turner
Ethel Watts Mumford
Eugene Sue
Eugenie Foa
Eugene Wood
Eustace Hale Ball
Evelyn Everett-green
Everard Cotes
F. H. Cheley
F. J. Cross
F. Marion Crawford
Fannie E. Newberry
Federick Austin Ogg
Ferdinand Ossendowski
Fergus Hume
Florence A. Kilpatrick
Fremont B. Deering
Francis Bacon
Francis Darwin
Frances Hodgson Burnett
Frances Parkinson Keyes
Frank Gee Patchin
Frank Harris
Frank Jewett Mather
Frank L. Packard
Frank V. Webster
Frederic Stewart Isham
Frederick Trevor Hill
Frederick Winslow Taylor

Friedrich Kerst
Friedrich Nietzsche
Fyodor Dostoyevsky
G.A. Henty
G.K. Chesterton
Gabrielle E. Jackson
Garrett P. Serviss
Gaston Leroux
George A. Warren
George Ade
Geroge Bernard Shaw
George Cary Eggleston
George Durston
George Ebers
George Eliot
George Gissing
George MacDonald
George Meredith
George Orwell
George Sylvester Viereck
George Tucker
George W. Cable
George Wharton James
Gertrude Atherton
Gordon Casserly
Grace E. King
Grace Gallatin
Grace Greenwood
Grant Allen
Guillermo A. Sherwell
Gulielma Zollinger
Gustav Flaubert
H. A. Cody
H. B. Irving
H.C. Bailey
H. G. Wells
H. H. Munro
H. Irving Hancock
H. R. Naylor
H. Rider Haggard
H. W. C. Davis
Haldeman Julius
Hall Caine
Hamilton Wright Mabie
Hans Christian Andersen
Harold Avery
Harold McGrath
Harriet Beecher Stowe
Harry Castlemon
Harry Coghill
Harry Houidini

Hayden Carruth
Helent Hunt Jackson
Helen Nicolay
Hendrik Conscience
Hendy David Thoreau
Henri Barbusse
Henrik Ibsen
Henry Adams
Henry Ford
Henry Frost
Henry James
Henry Jones Ford
Henry Seton Merriman
Henry W Longfellow
Herbert A. Giles
Herbert Carter
Herbert N. Casson
Herman Hesse
Hildegard G. Frey
Homer
Honore De Balzac
Horace B. Day
Horace Walpole
Horatio Alger Jr.
Howard Pyle
Howard R. Garis
Hugh Lofting
Hugh Walpole
Humphry Ward
Ian Maclaren
Inez Haynes Gillmore
Irving Bacheller
Isabel Cecilia Williams
Isabel Hornibrook
Israel Abrahams
Ivan Turgenev
J.G.Austin
J. Henri Fabre
J. M. Barrie
J. M. Walsh
J. Macdonald Oxley
J. R. Miller
J. S. Fletcher
J. S. Knowles
J. Storer Clouston
J. W. Duffield
Jack London
Jacob Abbott
James Allen
James Andrews
James Baldwin

James Branch Cabell
James DeMille
James Joyce
James Lane Allen
James Lane Allen
James Oliver Curwood
James Oppenheim
James Otis
James R. Driscoll
Jane Abbott
Jane Austen
Jane L. Stewart
Janet Aldridge
Jens Peter Jacobsen
Jerome K. Jerome
Jessie Graham Flower
John Buchan
John Burroughs
John Cournos
John F. Kennedy
John Gay
John Glasworthy
John Habberton
John Joy Bell
John Kendrick Bangs
John Milton
John Philip Sousa
John Taintor Foote
Jonas Lauritz Idemil Lie
Jonathan Swift
Joseph A. Altsheler
Joseph Carey
Joseph Conrad
Joseph E. Badger Jr
Joseph Hergesheimer
Joseph Jacobs
Jules Vernes
Julian Hawthrone
Julie A Lippmann
Justin Huntly McCarthy
Kakuzo Okakura
Karle Wilson Baker
Kate Chopin
Kenneth Grahame
Kenneth McGaffey
Kate Langley Bosher
Kate Langley Bosher
Katherine Cecil Thurston
Katherine Stokes
L. A. Abbot
L. T. Meade

L. Frank Baum
Latta Griswold
Laura Dent Crane
Laura Lee Hope
Laurence Housman
Lawrence Beasley
Leo Tolstoy
Leonid Andreyev
Lewis Carroll
Lewis Sperry Chafer
Lilian Bell
Lloyd Osbourne
Louis Hughes
Louis Joseph Vance
Louis Tracy
Louisa May Alcott
Lucy Fitch Perkins
Lucy Maud Montgomery
Luther Benson
Lydia Miller Middleton
Lyndon Orr
M. Corvus
M. H. Adams
Margaret E. Sangster
Margret Howth
Margaret Vandercook
Margaret W. Hungerford
Margret Penrose
Maria Edgeworth
Maria Thompson Daviess
Mariano Azuela
Marion Polk Angellotti
Mark Overton
Mark Twain
Mary Austin
Mary Catherine Crowley
Mary Cole
Mary Hastings Bradley
Mary Roberts Rinehart
Mary Rowlandson
M. Wollstonecraft Shelley
Maud Lindsay
Max Beerbohm
Myra Kelly
Nathaniel Hawthrone
Nicolo Machiavelli
O. F. Walton
Oscar Wilde

Owen Johnson
P.G. Wodehouse
Paul and Mabel Thorne
Paul G. Tomlinson
Paul Severing
Percy Brebner
Percy Keese Fitzhugh
Peter B. Kyne
Plato
Quincy Allen
R. Derby Holmes
R. L. Stevenson
R. S. Ball
Rabindranath Tagore
Rahul Alvares
Ralph Bonehill
Ralph Henry Barbour
Ralph Victor
Ralph Waldo Emmerson
Rene Descartes
Ray Cummings
Rex Beach
Rex E. Beach
Richard Harding Davis
Richard Jefferies
Richard Le Gallienne
Robert Barr
Robert Frost
Robert Gordon Anderson
Robert L. Drake
Robert Lansing
Robert Lynd
Robert Michael Ballantyne
Robert W. Chambers
Rosa Nouchette Carey
Rudyard Kipling
Saint Augustine
Samuel B. Allison
Samuel Hopkins Adams
Sarah Bernhardt
Sarah C. Hallowell
Selma Lagerlof
Sherwood Anderson
Sigmund Freud
Standish O'Grady
Stanley Weyman
Stella Benson
Stella M. Francis

Stephen Crane
Stewart Edward White
Stijn Streuvels
Swami Abhedananda
Swami Parmananda
T. S. Ackland
T. S. Arthur
The Princess Der Ling
Thomas A. Janvier
Thomas A Kempis
Thomas Anderton
Thomas Bailey Aldrich
Thomas Bulfinch
Thomas De Quincey
Thomas Dixon
Thomas H. Huxley
Thomas Hardy
Thomas More
Thornton W. Burgess
U. S. Grant
Upton Sinclair
Valentine Williams
Various Authors
Vaughan Kester
Victor Appleton
Victor G. Durham
Victoria Cross
Virginia Woolf
Wadsworth Camp
Walter Camp
Walter Scott
Washington Irving
Wilbur Lawton
Wilkie Collins
Willa Cather
Willard F. Baker
William Dean Howells
William le Queux
W. Makepeace Thackeray
William W. Walter
William Shakespeare
Winston Churchill
Yei Theodora Ozaki
Yogi Ramacharaka
Young E. Allison
Zane Grey

www.ingramcontent.com/pod-product-compliance
Lightning Source LLC
Chambersburg PA
CBHW031337170626
46807CB00002B/740

* 9 7 8 1 4 2 1 8 4 8 2 9 7 *